*To LET*
*My GOOD ... ENU*
*AND "NIGHT RIDER"*

# On the Fringe
# of the
# Real World

by

Robert Radez

PublishAmerica
Baltimore

Hardcover 9781448910687
Softcover 1424174503
eBook 9781462675500
PUBLISHED BY PUBLISHAMERICA, LLLP
www.publishamerica.com
Baltimore

Printed in the United States of America

# DEDICATION

From the time of my youth, as a small boy sitting in front of the living room console radio listening to Franklin D. Roosevelt and Winston Churchill, I've been deeply moved by the power of words. Truly amazing is how a seemingly insignificant simple sentence, not spoken by a world leader but offered by a friend in casual conversation, can, years later, shape one's decisions and life's direction. This book is dedicated to two such friends, John Raymond and Rose Berger.

John Raymond entered my life at a mid-career point in time when my direction was unsettled. Over the course of several conversations, John led me to realize and appreciate the uniqueness and strength of my God-given gifts to organize, manage and motivate people. The self-confidence that grew from John's support established a mindset of success that erased the normal human doubts and fear of failure. He became a mainstay in my business pursuits from that point, and remains a close friend.

Rose Berger was the Executive Secretary in my Woodland Hills, California sales office. Although I spent limited time with her personally, she had access to my various magazine articles and much of my business communications. During a casual conversation, speculating on what future activity I might consider after retirement, she argued with unusual conviction that writing should be my next pursuit. Even though it was already my intent to write several books, that advice, over time, crystallized my commitment to ignore the odds and begin this project.

# SPECIAL ACKNOWLEDGMENTS

Much of my generation has been largely left behind by the computer age. Beginning this project with very limited typing skills and almost no computer knowledge was a daunting task. Without the guiding hand and helpful encouragement of my good friend Debbie Descheemaeker, this effort may have led to total insanity rather than a completed book. I must also thank Debbie's husband (and my good golf buddy) Henrie, for his patience and support despite my routine interruptions of his life with yet more questions for Debbie. I will be eternally grateful for their friendship and unwavering support.

Some names have been changed to protect the guilty.

# CHAPTER ONE
## ~ Uncertainty ~

I loved Phoenix even before I set foot in it. Greeley's advice to "Go West, young man" had always had an enormous appeal to me.

As a boy, I had vicariously experienced many exciting adventures through the great epic westerns of Hollywood. The endless expanse and openness of the West infused me with a sense of freedom and wonder. The celluloid West portrayed by Hollywood was rife with excitement and limitless possibilities. Boyhood daydreams of living during this romanticized period of our history were not uncommon to me.

But this trip wasn't about living a dream. It was about escape and fulfilling a promise to myself. The further from Indianapolis we got, the better it felt.

The early morning darkness was surrendering to the first streaks of daylight as we drove into the Valley of the Sun, anxiety building as we neared the outskirts of the city. It had been 24 straight hours behind the wheel of my Olds "Super 88", U Haul in tow with all our belongings, my wife Judy and fourteen-month-old Debbie alternately providing company the whole way.

Cruising past miles of orange orchards, the morning air was saturated with the intoxicating scent of millions of orange blossoms, adding another sensory titillation to the breathtaking panorama unfolding before us. Most important, in the middle of that February, it was warm. The sun was making its much-touted daily appearance, and that, after all, was the impetus for this move.

True, I had been desperate to flee from what I thought was a stagnant path into a life of mediocrity. Only later in life would I come to realize it was not mediocrity from which I fled. It was normalcy. I couldn't have known, on that sun-blessed morning, that my life's future path would be far from "normal."

But it had been the cold—the seemingly inescapable cold—that fueled this decision to go west. That, and a promise I made to myself some four years prior. Now, virtually swimming in the warm, sweetly scented air of promise, my mind drifted freely to the uncomfortable events of the past, which had led me here. Memories of specific days, specific hours, specific pain, in Korea.

\* \* \*

As my graduation from high school had neared, I had taken notice of a growing number of slightly older friends and acquaintances whose newly developing lives, new jobs and meaningful relationships were abruptly disrupted by the draft into the armed services. Since I lacked both the genuine desire and the financial ability to attend college at that time, I chose to volunteer for the draft. It was my method to avoid disruption of established roots later on, as well as gaining the benefits of the G.I. bill. The added bonus—and it was huge—was the requirement to serve only two years instead of the four years required when enlisting. I was allowed to sign up for a chosen duty, and picked military police. After a quick basic training, I was assigned to the infantry as a rifleman and promptly shipped to Korea. So much for the military police.

A full strength infantry company at that time was made up of 190 men and six officers. About 100 of us who had been trained together were assigned to "C" company, 21st "Gimlet" Infantry Regiment, 24th Division, which had been decimated to 34 men and no officers when we arrived. I didn't need a Master's degree to figure out this was serious business. And it was cold.

The next couple months were spent in the snow. Running, walking, crawling, standing, sitting and sleeping in the snow. Running in the snow toward the North, then away from the North. Crunching up and down the mountain in the snow. Crawling into and out of bunkers and caves filled with snow. And sleeping—yes, sleeping—in the snow. I quit worrying about being shot and feared freezing to death.

Little did I realize the worst was yet to come.

My birthday that year was spent in a world of cold. My outfit was spread across the face of "Easy Block," a mountain position on the edge of the 38th parallel. We would spend several days in the area, mostly in the communications trenches, simple ditches some 5 feet deep, which connected the various observation and weapon's posts we manned. The nights were interminable nightmares of misery.

The cold became a test of will. It was a battle to maintain sanity. I stood in the communications trench, icy water gushing across my boots. My eyes strained against the pure blackness of the night, my mind racing between thoughts of freezing on this god-forsaken Korean mountainside and the prospects of living through one more night.

The hard freeze which plagued us for a week had lifted just enough that the blizzard had been transformed into falling mush and the accumulated snow was melting into a river of liquid ice that flowed through the trench. The mid-thirties temperatures assured that the constant flow of water through the trenches would remain virtually freezing.

We were in a "no light" zone, meaning no fires or lights of any kind. Even a lit match can be seen a mile away on a dark night. There was no escaping the cold. Several sleepless nights following days of crunching through the snow in pursuit of or retreat from the enemy had left me exhausted. I was aware of the hallucinations that distorted reality, further complicating the struggle to maintain my mental equilibrium. I had witnessed others in the preceding days who were unsuccessful in that struggle. They had simply lost it and crossed the line into some strange place called madness. It was terrible to see and downright frightening for a teenaged kid. But it strengthened my resolve to persevere and survive.

I needed to sleep. I had to sleep. Regardless of the circumstances and in utter defiance of the obvious, I made a decision, unsure whether it was insanity or sheer determination. I immersed my backpack down in the icy stream, placed my ammo belt on it and my canteen on top of that, creating a platform for my head above the water. My poncho had long since lost it's battle with the elements and I had been soaked to the skin for hours, but in my mind it would deflect the flow somewhat as I lay down, outstretched in the frigid stream, my head on the canteen, several inches above the surface of the rushing ice water. I forced myself to imagine it was not real, and somehow willed myself to sleep.

I wasn't sure I'd make it through that night, but I did. And I promised myself that if I survived that whole nightmare, I would never again subject myself to the cold. I'd had enough to last a lifetime.

\* \* \*

I was captured by the dramatic presence of Superstition Mountain, just several miles from Phoenix. The awe-inspiring vista combined with the morning warmth and sweet aromas drew me back into reality and left me feeling giddy. Maybe the 24 hours of highway hypnotism had something to do with it.

I felt an infusion of optimism and excitement spreading through my system. I knew Debbie was asleep on the makeshift bed I had rigged in the back seat, but I wasn't sure about Judy.

"Hon, you asleep?" I asked in a near whisper.

"I should be so lucky," came the immediate response. She pulled herself upright in the seat, gazing at the incredible scenery unfolding around us. "I don't know how I let you talk me into this," she said. "We don't know a soul here, you don't have a job, and we're just about broke... again. We should both have our heads examined. You and your damned 'I wanna go where the sun shines,'" she sneered.

My short-lived exuberance quickly evaporated. "Good Lord, Honey, how can you be so negative about everything? Just look at this fantastic new world around us. Take a deep whiff of this sweet, dry air. It's heavy with the promise of things to come. I'll find a job. I'll make some money. I'll make it happen."

Somehow I knew that no reasoning, no logic, no argument would convince her. We lived in different worlds. She was right about one thing; I was a dreamer, looking forward to what could be. But she was hung up on the pain of what had been. And since I was the cause of that pain, I was always sympathetic to her concern. Looking back, its clear we were doomed from the start.

\* \* \*

# CHAPTER TWO
## ~ Forks in the Road ~

It was summer in Indiana when I had shipped out of Korea and was discharged back into the real world. With my small separation pay from the Army, the little savings I had accumulated, and my Dad's help, I bought a bright red, '54 Ford convertible within a week. It was definitely play time. I now had the GI bill, but college could wait.

That's when I met Judy. She was beautiful. Tall, slender and blond, with all the pieces in the right places. Given the previous year of virtual isolation from anything resembling an American Beauty, combined with about 55 minutes of every hour imagining one, I was immediately hooked.

And I wasn't exactly chopped liver. My 6-foot frame carried a perfectly proportioned 175 pounds, in tremendous condition due to the rigorous physical demands of the previous two years. I had been blessed with attractive facial features since I was a boy, my Yugoslavian ancestry providing great genes. My outgoing Aquarian personality and gift of gab had always enabled me to easily gain favor with the opposite sex.

Judy and I wound up in a motel room on our third date. I was very inexperienced sexually, having lost my virginity a little over a year earlier just prior to shipping out to Korea. She too, displayed little knowledge in the sexual arena. That led to a wild and somewhat frenetic encounter. But it was a start.

Job wise, since I was living with my parents, I only needed enough money to pay a $51 monthly car payment and gas at 17 cents a gallon, a few beers and an occasional motel room at $6 or $7. It was a different world then. I went to work as a carpenter's helper for $1.50 per hour, pounding nails, sawing lumber and carrying 100-pound bundles of shingles up a ladder to the roof. Being typically macho, I decided to carry them two at a time. And that's exactly how I suffered the hernia, which led to my operation several weeks later.

It was in the recovery room, minutes after I regained consciousness from the operation, that Judy felt compelled to inform me that she was pregnant. She was panicked. I was stunned. Within minutes I said simply "We'll get married." Her panic immediately disappeared. So did my prospects for a college education.

* * *

I was emphatic—she would quit her job as a TWA stewardess, and she would be a great Mom. She reluctantly agreed. But when Debbie was born a whole new set of financial and other responsibilities began to take their toll. The bills began to pile up, and my $60 per week wasn't cutting it even though the rent on our apartment was only $60 a month.

I found a night gig selling vacuum cleaners. After a short training I began making house calls. With a $50 commission, I could nearly double my income with one sale per week. Within a couple weeks, I was averaging two sales each week, and we were beginning to catch up on the late payments. It did not escape my notice that in one hour of selling, I could make nearly the same money as a week of pounding nails. But I couldn't force myself to abandon the "sure money" of labor, and I fell into the trap that imprisons most Americans in a life of mediocrity.

Then came winter. I was offered a significant bonus to ignore the weather and help shingle the roof on a new home that was running behind schedule for completion. Hell, at that point, any additional monies were "significant." The pressures of reality dominated my life, and making money had become my obsession. I jumped at the chance.

So there I was, perched on the roof of this soon-to-be beautiful home in the middle of a large tree-covered lot in rural Indiana. And it was snowing. Hard. And it was cold. Very, very cold. The wind was howling and my hands could barely function. Even though I was as bundled up as practicality would allow, I was shivering, teeth chattering, cold to the bone.

Here I was again, right where I promised myself I would never be again. Only this time, I had a choice. I stood up, screaming in defiance into the blizzard that encompassed me, "FUCK YOU, FUCK THE SNOW, FUCK THE COLD, FUCK THIS JOB, FUCK THIS PLACE! I'M OUTTA HERE!"

With the icy conditions and blowing snow, it took me more than 90 minutes to drive the 15 miles from the job site to my home. Barging into the house, still angry with myself for my circumstances, I barked, "We're packing up and moving to Arizona." Judy was three months pregnant with our second baby, and her only sister was due to deliver her firstborn in some 60 days. Given that and the fact that we were beginning to see the possibility of normalcy in our lives, my proclamation was not warmly welcomed.

"What the hell are you talking about?"

In an exaggerated, slow enunciation of each syllable, I responded "We are moving to Arizona."

"I don't know what you've been smoking," she said defiantly, "but I'm not going anywhere."

"Your choice, but in ten days I'm loading what little we own in a U-Haul, Debbie and me in the car, and this bus is leaving town. You're my wife, the mother of my child, and your place is with me and the kids." I said it calmly but with authority and conviction. "Think about it."

A good 10 minutes elapsed before she spoke. "Who do you know in Arizona? What are you going to do there? For God's sake, Bob, have you ever even been there?"

"I don't know a soul there," I admitted. "I have no idea what I'm going to do there, and no, I've never been there. But by God, it's warm there all year round, and that's enough for starters."

I had never attempted to explain my life-altering experiences in Korea with her or anyone else. I knew it was impossible to convey the realities of such surreal conditions, and feared dredging up the images and related feelings, long since buried. But it was time to honor the promise I had made to myself.

By the time we left town ten days and hours of discussions later, trailer in tow, she had resigned herself to the trip. Understandably, she was not in accord with the decision.

\* \* \*

# CHAPTER THREE
## ~ The True Meaning of Broke ~

Phoenix was as warm and wonderful as I had imagined. I loved knowing that the sun would greet me every morning, and would rarely abandon me throughout the day. I loved the incredible desert landscape, the beautiful and multi-colored blossoms of the cacti in the spring, seeming to boast of vitality and endurance. I loved the regal bearing of the surrounding mountains that emphasized the Phoenix label of "Valley of the Sun." And the people of Phoenix seemed all to be from elsewhere, there by choice, not chance, and uniformly grateful about it. I loved it all.

Unfortunately, I was struggling to keep one step ahead of the bills. Actually, I was struggling to stay only one step behind. At that time, in the late 50's and early 60's, the economy of Phoenix revolved around tourism and construction. Unprecedented numbers of new residents were pouring in daily, fueling the housing market. "John Long Homes" was completing 100 houses per day, and "Hallcraft Homes" 25 per day. And buyers were added to a six months waiting list.

To stabilize our lives, I had joined the carpenter's union shortly after our arrival in town. Frankly, I wasn't qualified, but I needed only to pass an oral test to join. While my carpentering skills may have been minimal, my skills at bullshit dispensing were extraordinary—and that carried the day. I became the youngest journeyman ever to join the Phoenix union.

In the following months, I was confronted with how little I really knew about carpentering. Fortunately, the huge building boom provided enough job opportunities that eventually the union would come up with something so simple even I could do it.

Like most families in our age group at that time, we lived from paycheck to paycheck. But in less than two years we were able to buy our first home, one of the Hallcraft models on the northwest outskirts of town, a bedroom community of mostly young families like ours.

Our family had grown in the two years since we had arrived. Mark and Mike had entered the world only one year apart. We had quickly outgrown the little rental house in the desert, some eight miles north of Sunnyslope—the northernmost boundary of Phoenix at the time—and were thrilled with our new home. Three bedrooms, two and ½ baths, red brick home with cedar shake shingles, double car garage with ample storage space, surrounded by a fully landscaped lot with palm and citrus trees and a nice yard for the kids. All for $12,050 dollars!

My G I bill enabled me to buy the home with no down payment, $100 closing costs, and a 4 1/4% loan. Truly, it was a different world back then.

One would think that with each step forward in our lives—real job, paychecks, three wonderful kids and a new home—Judy and I would be growing closer. To the contrary, optimism remained a foreign concept to Judy. In one typical gut-wrenching harangue, she revealed one of the hidden thorns causing her ongoing pain: she couldn't get past the belief that I was resentful of Debbie's birth. I became convinced she relished her misery. It was the only thing that pleased her. She had become and remained cold and distant. Only our kids kept us together.

In contrast to Judy, I found it relatively easy to remain optimistic. I simply compared where I was to where I had been. Three years earlier we had been broke, really broke. Or so I thought. I would soon learn the true meaning of "broke."

\* \* \*

It started with a labor strike by the engineers. In construction, everything starts with the engineers. The initial stages of ground clearing and preparation as well as the structural foundations are in their hands. With the engineers on strike, very soon no foundations are being laid. Without foundations, new buildings cannot start. Eventually, all started projects are finished and all work dries up. That's exactly what happened in Phoenix in 1960. The construction industry accounted for such a large part of the city's economy, that within a couple months, with no labor settlement in sight, the entire city became strangled economically. The ripple effect damaged nearly every kind of business in the Valley. Major grocery chains were laying off personnel and shortening business hours. Many businesses closed. Virtually everyone was negatively affected. Living paycheck to paycheck, a financial avalanche rapidly overwhelmed us, carrying us downward in its momentum toward an unknown fate.

Since my experience of selling vacuum sweepers in Indianapolis, I had always considered commissioned sales as my ace in the hole. In fact, only Judy's insistence on the sure (if small) weekly check kept me from pursuing a sales career; one of my concessions to a civil relationship.

A friend once told me that if you looked hard enough, you would find the word "security" tattooed on every woman's forehead. I'm sure there are exceptions, but in general, time does make the tattoo seem more prominent. It's part of the "nesting" instinct in women. Judy simply could not accept the risk side of the "risk/reward" concept.

I was greatly enamored of earnings being limited only by one's ability and/ or production. To me it seemed clear: in sales the harder you worked, the more you sold; the more you sold, the more you earned; the more you earned, the more motivated you became; the more motivated, the harder you worked; the harder you work…. well, that's a merry-go-round that made sense. Especially when it provided the chance for the golden ring. I knew I would never grab a golden ring swinging a hammer.

I drifted from one sales job to another, trying to find a product that could be sold in a financially devastated community. I was able only to grind out enough commissions to feed the family—and that very poorly. We had fallen a couple months behind on the mortgage, and I was receiving nasty letters from GMAC about the loan on my new Chevy. That's when I met Bill. I had followed up on an ad for "seasoned sales pros." I attended a meeting to get more information on the deal and there, among the guys who showed up, I met and began what would be a lifetime friendship with Bill Hunter.

### ~ Necessity Is a Mother ~

He was a couple inches shorter than I, very blond, somewhat uncoordinated and unathletic and seemingly reserved—virtually no commonalities. However, as we began to get acquainted, I found we had much in common.

He too was totally busted and desperate.

His three kids were nearly identical in age to mine.

He was facing foreclosure on his house.

Like me, he had grown up in a strict Catholic family but had drifted away from the church.

He'd married at 19 for the same reason as I and had struggled with the realities of life ever since. A meaningful bond quickly developed. Over the next few months, Bill and I worked various sales gigs—sometimes together, sometimes not—looking for the "winner" and comparing notes regularly. We came to recognize two distinctly different worlds; the "real" world with real people who had real jobs and real lives. And our world, on the fringe of the real world, surreal and uncertain, fraught with perils unknown to the real people in the real world.

We needed money desperately and nothing was working out. We determined that there were evil gremlins on the fringe, assigned to screw with our lives. Random chance couldn't possibly govern all the failures we were encountering. It had to be "THEM". "THEY" were in control of our fate. We were only half kidding.

Bill and his family were evicted. With his charming personality and sincerity -and a hot check- he was able to rent a little house on the wrong side of Tempe, southeast of the city. This put us on opposite ends of our metropolitan area universe. Since their furniture had already been repossessed, the kitchen table, chairs and the few other pieces of furniture in the rental home were a godsend for his family.

The NSF check had become standard operating procedure: write the check knowing you had several days "float" time to dig up the money and get it in the bank before the check hit. Sometimes it worked; sometimes it didn't. But his family was off the street.

I was two or three months behind on my mortgage, but my GI loan afforded me more slack than usual. My power had been shut off periodically, usually when I was unable to cover the check I had written to keep it on. But Bill's power had been off for over a month when we met one afternoon in Encanto Park, a central location, to commiserate with each other.

As depressed as I was with my circumstances, I felt even worse for Bill. I would have given him the shirt off my back. However, like me, he didn't need a shirt. He needed money. A dollar was worth something then, but I didn't have one.

"For God's sake Bill, how are you guys making it without any power."

"Charcoal," he said, "And Margaret." Margaret, his devoted wife, was an unwavering supporter of Bill, no matter what. Given the circumstances, I was in awe of her willingness to do whatever she could for the cause.

"Margaret found a job waiting tables," he said dejectedly, "so we're hoping to get enough money together in a few days to get the power turned on. They won't take my checks anymore." "What about the charcoal?" I asked.

"We're doing all our cooking on the charcoal grill." He paused a moment, in thought, then continued, as if in surrender, "Bob, let me tell you the worst. Of course, it's all a goddamn nightmare. But the absolute pits is when I'm out in the yard at 4 AM to light the charcoal so I can heat the grill and brew some coffee on it before the neighbors get up and see me."

I was stunned. "Holy horseshit" I muttered, realizing that I was only days away from a similar fate. As bad off as I was, there was still room to fall. Many talk of being broke. But this …. THIS was broke. Really, truly, fucking broke. I sat in silence, contemplating the picture just painted by Bill. It was so absurd it was funny. I couldn't stifle the chuckle, which quickly grew into an all out laugh. Bill knew I was viewing the visual he had just created, and soon both of us were lost in laughter. It was a much-needed temporary lifeboat. We were both treading water in a tsunami of desperation. But the seriousness of our reality painfully reinserted itself. When it did, I quickly sobered up and found my voice. "Bill, we have to find a way out of this. Legal, illegal, moral or immoral, I don't give a shit. We have to come up with something now."

"We've tried selling about everything. What's left?" He pondered.

We sat in thought for a time. "You know, Bill, we've met a lot of people in the past several months. Who do we know that has expressed some dream? If we knew in advance what someone wanted, maybe we could come up with a way to sell it to them. Or scam it. Whatever."

"Wait a minute," Bill exclaimed. "The dream is the thing. And I do know a guy who has one—big time. About a year ago, before we met, I decided to open a detective business. Here in Arizona all you have to do to be a private detective is hang up a shingle that says "Detective" and you are one. No license, no nothing. So I put an ad in the paper for clients. A guy shows up who wants to work for me. Really strange guy; forty something, still living with his mother, claims he has all the credentials for 'expert detective' and virtually begs me to hire him; says he's wanted to be a private eye all his life. But as strange as the guy was, he had an address on the north side in a real high-end exclusive neighborhood. I may still have his name and number somewhere."

Bill found the number and within hours we made an appointment to meet with the guy in his home regarding a unique, once in a lifetime opportunity. With less than an hour prior to the meeting we concocted our plan: Bill would introduce me as a former, highly acclaimed private detective from the Pinkerton's Private Detective agency in Indianapolis. The story: I had recently resigned to open a state of the art agency in rapidly growing Phoenix, and had sought out Bill as a "Senior Partner" due to his local expertise. Now we were interviewing interested parties for a "Junior Partnership" in the firm. Of course we wanted a capable person serious enough to have a vested interest in the business, requiring a small investment.

We spent very little time smoothing out our story and decided to play it by ear, trusting our abilities to shoot from the hip. Just in case we were able to pique his interest to the investing stage, we planned to strengthen the pitch with a "take-away".

In sales parlance, the take-away is akin to setting the hook when the fish bites. Since we all have a natural resistance to being sold, a seasoned pro will, upon detecting a prospective buyer's genuine interest in the offer, decline to sell it to the buyer for some imaginary reason, almost irresistibly whetting the prospect's desire to buy. This technique is usually employed only by the strongest of the strong, since less experienced sales people usually try to close the deal at the first sign of acceptance by the buyer. The take-away, properly executed, results in the buyer aggressively pursuing the deal rather than passively accepting the deal. Particularly if the deal is a scam, you don't want to seem anxious to get the money. Frankly, ours was a semi-scam—we intended to actually open the agency if successful in scamming the money.

\* \* \*

Our "mark" seemed very anxious to discuss our proposition, asking that we meet with him that day. It was slightly before the 3 PM meeting time when we pulled into his driveway. The home was a magnificent sprawling brick one-story ranch home, surrounded by an orange grove. It was located just a couple blocks off of North Central Avenue on the outskirts of Phoenix, without a doubt the most upscale area in town at that time. There was a long tunnel-like trellised walkway leading from the driveway to the front door. I'm sure Bill was as nervous as I when we knocked on the door, no idea what may be in store for us.

The door abruptly swung wide open and a most imposing figure stood before us. He stood some six-feet tall but appeared much larger due to his big-boned frame. His huge square face resembled a recently sculpted clay bust, a work in progress, still rough and bumpy in places. His 220-pound frame was clothed in impeccable tan slacks and a dress shirt, his chest hair pouring from the unbuttoned top of the shirt. He could easily have been mistaken for a pro football player. His deep booming voice was unnerving as he bellowed " Good to see you again, Bill", while extending his huge paw of a hand out to Hunter.

"Bill Hodgkins, I want you to meet Bob Radez, a business associate of mine" said Hunter. His hand engulfed mine in a frighteningly intense grip and shake.

"Bill told me of you, and I'm really excited to meet you," he exclaimed, his voice a gravely imitation of James Earl Jones. We were to find out later that Hodgkins disease was named after his grandfather, an eminent physician who had identified the disease years prior.

Hodgkins led us down a narrow hallway that emptied out into a spacious sunken living room. The spotless, white carpet was the perfect setting for the obviously expensive furniture. The entire room and its trappings reeked of wealth. He motioned us into two easy chairs and positioned himself on an ottoman facing us.

Even the initial small talk indicated that Hodgkins was already predisposed to a deal. Hunter and I had agreed that I would begin the presentation with Hunter being an observer to clean up any inconsistencies or glaring contradictions I might commit. This was, after all, a totally unrehearsed, play-by-ear ad-lib.

I related with growing enthusiasm my imaginary deep experience as a private detective; our plans for the business; our unspecified, but of course, substantial financial commitment; the office (non-existent) on McDowell Road and other flights of fancy.

"Hodgkins—may I call you Hodgkins?—an operation of this scope will require the involvement of absolutely top quality personnel, and we want to have someone with a vested interest in the operation, same as us. A Junior Partner." I then set up the takeaway. "We're only *interviewing* interested applicants at this time, and we've narrowed the field down to the three most qualified men in this area. Of course, Hodgkins, you are one of those three."

Hunter then took over for the "interview", with me as observer. What we heard from Hodgkins in the next 30 minutes was beyond unbelievable.

At the onset of the interview, Hodgkins made a quick trip to his bedroom to retrieve several framed "diplomas", each certifying him in some specific aspect of sleuth expertise.

* He had one for "handcuffing", another for "stakeouts".

*Yet another diploma for "tailing," although he had no car, no drivers license.

He "earned" them through courses offered in the back of various "Crime" magazines.

* Asked how he tailed targeted subjects, he said with total conviction that he had studied the city bus schedule, and could seamlessly make needed connections. He pointed out that by using the buses, he was less likely to be spotted by the subject.

* He knew how to drive, but the State of Arizona had refused to issue a license to him since his brief stay at the Arizona sanitarium. He pointed out how grossly unfair this was since he had a document signed by the Governor attesting to his sanity, provided on his release from the State hospital. He said, "I have written proof of my sanity. Do you?"

* He was 44 years old, never married. We found out later, he'd never been on a date, although he claimed to have "… completed the ceremony …"in the bushes outside of church one glorious evening years before.

"So how much is this Junior Partnership going to cost?" He directed the question to me.

I had been so mesmerized with the absurdity of his responses, that I was taken totally off-guard. Not until that moment did I realize Hunter and I had never discussed an amount to shoot for. My mind went blank, and I immediately felt panic surge through my body.

Out of the blue I heard Hunter calmly respond, "$10,000. Cash"

When that figure finally sunk into my clouded brain, I nearly fainted. My God, I thought, that's more than the average annual income. Hell, that was probably 10 times my current year's income. New Cadillacs were selling at that time for $5000.

Hunter had lost his mind. I would have thought in terms of a thousand or two. I was reeling from shock, but not Hodgkins. Without any hesitation, he jumped at it.

"I can put that together in a day or two." He was emphatic. He was clearly growing hyper, his excitement beginning to escape all containment.

The whole meeting had become incredibly surreal. We had come to con Bill Hodgkins out of some money. It was now obvious that Bill Hodgkins was doing his best to con us into taking it. With each passing moment Hodgkins became more excited and more impassioned. The picture was now totally in focus—he had spent most of his life dreaming of being a private eye, and here it was, in his grasp. It was time to set the hook, although in reality, our fish was trying desperately to jump in the boat.

Buoyed by the positive response from Hodgkins, I continued with the next step of the take-away. "No, no, Bill. We're not ready to make a decision yet. In fact, we still have one other person to interview over in Scottsdale. We have an appointment with him in 30 minutes. We just want to find the best candidate for the position."

Hodgkins was adamant. And growing very antsy. "OK, maybe I can get the money together sooner." he pleaded. Hunter and I both began to assure him this had nothing to do with money.

"Hodgkins" I barked at him, hoping to settle him down. "If you offered us the money right now it wouldn't matter. We're shopping for the man, not the money."

He wasn't buying it. Becoming somewhat hysterical, he was obviously coming unwound. "You're just gonna see if someone else can get you the money before I can," he bellowed. Our assurances to the contrary had no effect on him.

Suddenly, this gorilla of a man jumped to his feet, fists clenched, head tilted back, then let out an unworldly roar. "AARRAAAAAAAGH". It seemed to go on forever. I was frozen in my tracks. I had no idea how Hunter was reacting because I couldn't tear my bug-eyed fix off the roaring beast five feet in front of me.

Then, just as suddenly as it had begun, it stopped. He was still in the rigid position, but the howl had been replaced by an eerie whistling; short one-second bursts "tweeeet, tweeeet, tweeeet". Hunter and I sat there, frozen in shock. Then we saw it. The dark stain beginning in the crotch of his tan slacks and spreading rapidly down the legs. He was pissing his pants while whistling, seemingly in some sort of trance.

My legs operated independently of my shell-shocked brain and I found myself moving very quickly toward the hallway leading to the front door. Hunter was on the same path, also somewhat brain-numbed, and we began crashing into each other in the narrow hallway, both in a full-out flight pattern.

We somehow made it through the door and scrambled for the car. I was trembling as I floored the big-block Chevy out of the neighborhood and down Central Avenue toward nowhere in particular. We had 60 cents between us, and decided to blow a dime apiece on a cup of java to settle our nerves at the coffee shop at McDowell Road and Central.

At the counter, nursing my coffee, I was trying to stop my hands from shaking. "Good Lord, Bill, what the hell was that?"

Hunter was spilling his coffee as his motor skills had also apparently short-circuited. "Jesus, Bob, what have we gotten ourselves into?" he moaned.

"Well, it's pretty obvious this guy had an abnormal desire to get involved with us," I began to reason, attempting to rationally evaluate the situation. "This guy may be a whack job, but he's dreamed of this moment all his life, and just when he thought he had it, we jerked it away from him".

"Hey, man," Hunter said, the color returning to his face, "I'll bet we're the only guys in history that laid a take-away so strong that when the buyer found out he couldn't have it, he pissed his pants and whistled about it." It was funny, but neither of us could muster a laugh.

I was now thinking of the effect of our encounter on Hodgkins and a scary thought hit me. "Bill, what do you think he's doing right now?"

Bill thought for a few seconds, then in a semi-whisper replied. "My God, Bob, he's in the basement hanging himself."

A sick feeling was starting to spread through my gut. "That's exactly what I was thinking. What the hell are we gonna do about it?"

We figured we would have to invent a reason to call him, and if he didn't answer, we'd send an emergency vehicle there.

But what if he did answer?

Well, we'd feel out his mood, tell him the other applicant stood us up, and then offer the partnership to Hodgkins. We flipped a coin. The winner had to pay the nickel for the call; the looser had to make the call.

Hunter lost the toss. We shared the earpiece. Again, we were in for a surprise.

Neither of us expected an answer. "Hello" came the deep, totally calm, unmistakable voice of Bill Hodgkins.

"Uhh, uhh, Bill. This is Bill Hunter."

"Yes Bill, good to hear from you. What's up?"

Hunter, visibly unnerved, darted a puzzled look at me. "I'm calling to let you know that our other applicant showed up quite late for our appointment, and we don't want to get in bed with an unreliable sort. Do you still have an interest?"

"Absolutely." The answer was immediate and again emphatic. "I have to sell some securities in the morning to raise the cash, but could probably meet you around 2 PM tomorrow. Will that work for you?"

"That'll be just fine Bill. Meet us … at the coffee shop on McDowell and Central tomorrow at 2 PM."

"I'll see you there," said Hodgkins.

Hunter hung up the receiver and looked at me for a good minute before speaking. "What the hell is going on?" Hodgkins hadn't even mentioned the fiasco that had shocked us to the core only minutes prior. How the hell could he be so calm and business-like after what had taken place?

Now we became suspicious. "Bill, am I just paranoid, or does this smell like a set-up?"

"Bob, my mind is so damned warped right now I don't know what to think. It's scary as hell, but I can't get past the ten grand. If it's a set-up, what could he do?"

"Well, it's pretty obvious he's not all there. God only knows what he's thinking. He could shoot us. Or just kick your ass while I run for help." I could still picture him towering over me, his unearthly growl permeating his living room as my fight or flight instinct made a definite decision.

"Look Bob, the bottom line is we're going to be here at two o'clock tomorrow. The reward outweighs the risk. So let's get it together and be prepared to make it work out."

As we slowly calmed down, we began to make plans for the ten grand. Plans beyond our rent, car payments and utilities. But those would come off the top. What were the odds?

Early the next morning, we were shopping for upscale apartments on McDowell Road where we had alluded to having an office. We made arrangements to rent an impressive apartment, agreeing to finalize the transaction that afternoon and have the furniture removed from one of the two bedrooms. We then made a similar delayed action arrangement for rental office furniture to be delivered later in the day. By the 2 PM moment of truth, we had everything in place to have a respectable looking office by that evening.

Hunter and I went together to meet Hodgkins at the coffee shop. Both of us were resigned to face the music if this deal backfired. At precisely 2 PM, Hodgkins walked through the restaurant door, made his way straight to our booth, said hello, sat down and laid 100 hundred-dollar bills on the table.

"When do I start?" he growled.

Hunter had worked the previous night composing a reasonable looking document that gave Hodgkins a 20% interest in the agency. It was intentionally complicated, allowing me the time to excuse myself with the money.

"We can't let this money sit here in plain sight. I'll run it down to the bank. You fellows take care of the paperwork, and when I get back, we'll go to the office."

It actually worked out. I zoomed to the apartment complex and completed the rental agreement and while the bedroom furniture was being removed, I was arranging for the office furniture to be delivered in its place. By nightfall, we had a relatively functional-looking office, and one very excited Junior Partner. "Arizona Confidential" was born.

We told Hodgkins our printing would be done in a few days, and that we had been told of a substantial waiting time to have our phones installed. He said he had an uncle at the main telephone office and could probably get the phones installed pronto. The three of us made the trip and sure enough, his uncle, although visibly puzzled, arranged for near immediate installation.

The ride back to the office was not as smooth. The excitement of the success he had accomplished at the phone company combined with the reality that he was now a bona-fide private eye was too much for Hodgkins. He suddenly stiffened, eyes rolling into the back of his head, and then he let go with what would become a familiar roar, fading into the whistle routine. And yes, he pissed himself again, in the front seat of my car.

Afterward, we found he had no recollection of the "fit" other than his pants were wet. Intent on getting to the bottom of this, we made some serious inquiries. Hodgkins revealed that he had quit taking his prescribed medication because he "…no longer had the epileptic seizures experienced in the past." Finally, the whole unbelievable episode began to make sense.

I had no way of knowing that this was to be only the first in a series of bizarre episodes and unusual characters that would weave a strange fabric of life on the fringe of "the real world." It was to be a wild ride, fraught with difficulties. But it would not be dull.

\* \* \*

# CHAPTER FOUR
## ~ Close but No Cigar ~

You couldn't call it "flourishing" but the agency, Arizona Confidential, was paying the bills. Hodgkins' "investment" had enabled both Bill and I to bring all our debt current as well as fund the initial expenses of the agency. A few simple ads in the Arizona daily had generated a sporadic flow of clients, keeping the rent paid and the lights on. While it was nothing to hoot about, the situation was a major improvement from where we were some four months earlier, before the Hodgkins era began.

Fortunately, most of our cases were simple matters, usually marital problems requiring surveillance of a suspected spouse. Keeping someone under constant watch 24 hours a day, recording precisely where and when they went and with whom they met can be tedious and boring. But such jobs allowed us to hone our skills, and most of the cases were uncomplicated enough that we could handle them ourselves without outside help. Occasionally, however, an exception to the commonplace would come to us.

She was mid-thirties, nicely dressed and well mannered when she walked into our office unannounced. After introducing ourselves, Hunter and I sat opposite her in a comfortable living room arrangement we had designed for client interviews, away from the desk and office environment. As had become the norm, we sat on the couch, relaxed but attentive to our client who sat nervously across the coffee table in a comfortable chair.

"Gentlemen," she began apologetically, "I'm sorry if I'm wasting your time, but I really don't know where to go for help."

"Mrs. Bartell, you're not obligated for anything here," I assured her. "Just relax and tell us your problem and we'll decide whether we can help you."

"Well, it's my son, David. He's fourteen. He met an older fellow named Kenny; thirtyish I'd guess, in the park. Kenny seems pretty effeminate, and at twice David's age, his intentions are questionable. I've tried to dissuade David from spending time with this guy, but the harder I try to discourage him, the more persistent he becomes. Today, David informed me he was going to leave home for the summer and live with this Kenny.

"I put my foot down and forbade him to leave, but he became downright hostile. He's bigger than me already and I was frightened of my own son. He grabbed some clothes and when I blocked the door, demanding he stay, he shoved me aside violently and told me he'd hurt me if I tried to stop him. I'm at wits end and don't know what to do. I was just sitting at my kitchen table crying my eyes out, and happened on your ad. Do you think you can help? And what would this cost?"

"Do you know where this Kenny lives?" Hunter asked.

"Yes, he has a house just a couple blocks away from mine."

I could tell Hunter was warming to the challenge. "Exactly what would you like to see happen?"

"I just want David to come home. Well, I guess I really want to convince him that his behavior in unacceptable. "

Hunter leaned forward and in a very personal and assuring manner explained, "Mrs. Bartell, we normally charge a standard hourly fee plus expenses for our services. But I'm confident I can solve your problem and will handle it for a flat $100 fee so you won't have to wonder what it'll end up costing you."

"May I ask how you intend to accomplish this?"

"I will personally persuade Kenny it's the right thing to do."

"If I agree, when can you do this?"

"Today," was Hunter's answer. "We wouldn't want your boy to spend the night there, now would we?"

She seemed somewhat relieved if not convinced, cut us a check for the hundred, thanked us for our help and departed.

Hodgkins bolted from the spare bedroom where he had been eavesdropping. "I'll go with you Bill, just in case. Backup, you know?"

Bill told him that he appreciated his offer, but that this was a one-man job.

Hodgkins put in his standard mild protest, then reluctantly agreed, and went about his business.

We had found out with our first potential client that Hodge—as we came to refer to him—could not be present for client interviews.

Present with Bill and I during that initial interview, he became more and more excited and finally exploded into what we then knew was a seizure, all in full view of the totally stunned woman, who ran from the office when she was finally able to recover from the initial shock.

But as we became more aware of his condition, we were more able to accommodate him in the environment. We were successful in persuading him to begin his medications again, and after the first six or eight client interviews, he was able to control his emotions and avoid the seizures at such occasions. Even so, we made sure he remained in the adjoining room as a precaution.

Hodge was a mainstay in the office, taking full interest in everything that transpired. While he couldn't actually pursue any operative roles, we would take him along for stakeouts and other non-contact duties. He was a likeable, easy-going guy, and we treated him as a partner, even though to our clients he may have been a hidden, silent partner. He literally lived for this. The ins and outs of Arizona Confidential were his reason for existence. In fact, a tense, unexpected standoff with his sister led to a remarkable revelation.

Kate was a very intelligent sort, a legal aide in a prestigious Phoenix law firm. Two months after Hodge had cashed out some securities for his Junior Partnership, she discovered the transaction and went berserk, suspecting for some strange reason that we had taken advantage of her brother. OK, so maybe we had. But he had received basically what we promised. Since she viewed him as incompetent, somewhat retarded as well as struggling with epilepsy, she was confident there could be no legitimate role for him in a reputable business. She concluded we must have been bilking him. Why else keep him around? And she let us know it in no uncertain terms.

One Monday morning she tore into our office and began ripping Bill and I unmercifully in Hodge's presence. "I'm on to you, and you bastards will not get away with this. What kind of smarmy assholes would rip off a sick retard? God only knows how much more you've bilked from him since this started, but you're going to return it all—and I mean now. I've got connections all over this city, and by God, if you don't end this farce and give him back what you've stolen, I'll see to it you're both in a jail cell by tonight. "

Before we had a chance to defend ourselves, Hodge jumped in with both feet, condemning her for the outrageous charges and bragging about the money he had earned, fortunately not mentioning the embarrassingly anemic amount of said earnings. Kate dismissed his every word as evidence of his continuing lunacy and continued issuing threats with each new sentence.

I have never seen Bill Hunter naked, but he must have the balls of a rhinoceros. He pulled a piece of paper from the desk, jotted something on it, signed it and calmly handed it to Hodge.

"Lady, you have no idea what you're talking about, or the terrible disservice you're attempting to force on your brother. To try to prevent you from doing more harm to him than you've already done, I've giving him an IOU for his initial investment, the only monies he has put into this business. As it clearly states, its payable on demand. He can cash out any time he chooses from this minute on, but it will be at his choosing."

We didn't have $50 in the bank or $10 cash between us. What Hunter did was both an enormous risk and a brilliant ploy. I had felt since Korea that I could face anything, but I doubt I could have pulled the trigger on that one. It took a serious gamblers heart and Hunter had read the hand perfectly. Hodge looked at the IOU for a moment. It seemed like an eternity. Then he theatrically ripped it into shreds and threw them into his sister's face. She sputtered momentarily, then stormed out of the office. And through it all, Hodge did not have a seizure.

We were all jubilant—like three ten-year olds whose tree house had withstood a major storm. And once again, I was enormously impressed by my friend, Bill Hunter.

The next day, we were very comforted and moved emotionally by a phone call from Hodge's Mother. Kate had related to her the matter of the previous day's meeting with us, and she wanted us to know that we would never again hear from her daughter. She said she had let Kate know the reality of the situation: Hodge had never had a job, never had a friend, never had a place to go, and never had anything to look forward to. For the first time in his life, he now had them all. And for the first time in his life, he was truly happy. She made it clear to her daughter and now wanted us to know that we were the greatest thing to ever happen in his life, and she would be eternally grateful for our involvement with her son.

Some consequences in life are too strange to even attempt explanation.

\* \* \*

## ~ The Art of Persuasion ~

Hunter knocked on the screen door. Before home air-conditioners became the norm, doors were commonly left open, and only a screen door separated inside from outside. As the young man inside approached to answer, Bill could see 14-year-old David in the background, hesitantly peering through the screen at the stranger.

"Yes?" he asked.

"Are you Kenny?"

"Uhhh, yes."

The slightly lisped answer had barely escaped his lips when Hunter's right hand exploded through the screen door, violently grabbing Kenny by the neck. In one snatch Hunter jerked him through the screen and onto the porch. Kenny was immediately slammed into the wall. There he dangled, seemingly impaled by Hunter's unrelenting grip on his throat. He could barely breath and was writhing in pain as Hunter, now nose to nose, said slowly and distinctly, " When I let you go, you are going to walk—or crawl—back into the house. You will convince the kid he is no longer welcome, tell him he needs to be leaving in one minute and going straight home. You're also going to make it very clear that he will never even think about coming back and you will promise him that if he does, you will personally slap the living shit out of him. And if any of this doesn't happen, I'm going to revisit you with a couple very large friends who aren't as sweet and tolerant of mistakes as I am, and would just love to know where you live. Am I making myself clear?"

Hunter could feel the attempted nod, but the vice-like grip made speech or movement of the head impossible. His release was immediately followed by a huge gasp for air. Kenney wasted no time beginning the task at hand. Hunter waited at the door, and within seconds the kid emerged, clothes in hand, and began to run flat out for home. David had, of course, heard it all.

Several days later, Mrs. Bartell called to thank Bill and say the kid had a much-improved attitude. We never heard from her again.

\* \* \*

Our chance at the gold ring was courtesy of a neighbor in the apartment building, which housed our office. She was a good looking and friendly woman, maybe pushing 40. We spent much of our down time at the pool, and over the weeks had chatted with her on several occasions.

One afternoon she told us she had a close friend who wanted to find a very discreet private detective agency. We assured her that we fit the description. She passed along the info to her friend, and he called a few days later. He said simply his name was John, as in John Doe, and asked to meet us at his office The directions to his place really got our attention.

He was a co-owner of the Shadows Resort, possibly the most exclusive, luxurious, expensive and famous resort in the area. Located on the backside of Camelback Mountain, his was a favorite getaway for many of Hollywood's biggest names.

He had a stunningly gorgeous girlfriend, Tina, whom he showered with generosity. He housed her in one of the most expensive poolside suites in the resort. He had come to suspect she was entertaining some guy in the room and wanted to know if such damning information he had received was accurate. John, attempting to be reasonable about his concerns, expressed no interest in what she did off the property, and did not want her followed, but was extremely upset over the prospect of her indiscretions at his expense in the accommodations he provided.

He wanted the room under surveillance 24 hours a day for a week or so, with accurate records of all people entering and leaving. However, she absolutely was not to know of the surveillance.

Since Bill and I would be seen occasionally visiting his office, he did not want us personally involved in the surveillance. He was taking no chances of her putting two and two together, just in case she was clean. We were to report to him personally every other day, and he would pay us in cash each time. He also gave us our required retainer.

This was big time. This was big bucks. A client like this could turn our agency into a major player in the right circles. It would require several operatives trading off at various times during the day while posing as sun worshipers at the pool. We would be expanding our operations immediately.

The job started in earnest on a Saturday morning, and by noon we already had our first glitch. Sally was a top operative for us and was to be on poolside duty till 4 PM. At noon she contacted Bill to notify him that she would have to leave before her shift was up. She had overlooked a previous commitment to pick up her fiancée at the airport at 3 PM, and would have to leave no later than 2 PM. Bill would have to find someone to cover.

Cell phones had yet to be dreamed of and being out of touch, especially on a Saturday, was common. Bill began calling around but was having no luck.

As the time ticked by he began to panic. Soon, he was out of options. Except one.

As always, Hodge was there, monitoring the disaster in the making.

"Send me, Bill. I can handle it." It was at least the tenth time he had pleaded his case. Only now, Bill actually began to consider it. He knew Hodge might just be his only hope to prevent blowing our dream client out of the water on the first day of our contract. He was trying to determine the lesser of the two potential disasters. Finally, out of time and with a totally rational Hodge nipping at his heels, he sat down facing Hodge, their noses some 3 feet apart. He looked Hodge dead in the eyes and began in a slow, serious tone.

"Hodge, listen to me closely. Sally is on surveillance duty at the Shadows Resort, but she has to go to Sky Harbor Airport and pick up someone, so I'm going to assign you to take a cab out to the resort, relieve Sally and take up her surveillance of room # 101 at the pool. Just act like you're reading a magazine and make notes on anyone going in or out of the room. That's all we care about, OK? You'll only be there a couple hours till the 4 PM operative arrives. Then take a cab back to the office. Got it?"

"Got it" came the immediate reply.

"Any questions?" asked Bill, already starting to feel a little queasy.

"None." Bill could hear the combination of enthusiasm and excitement in the response. He paused, realizing this was certainly risky if not insane. But how bad could it be? What could possibly happen worse than jeopardizing the project? Many questions raced through his head, but, out of time and options, he called for the cab.

Both were extremely anxious as the taxi rolled up, but for different reasons. The concerns swimming in Bill's head were only compounded when Hodge jumped in the car and shouted to the driver, "Sky Harbor Airport."

In stunned disbelief, Bill was screaming at the now departing taxi, finally getting the attention of the driver. He snatched open the door and moaned "For God's sake Hodge, you're going to the Shadows Resort to relieve Sally. Remember?"

"Sure, Bill. No problem. Shadows Resort, driver."

As the taxi pulled away again, the words were ricocheting in Bill's brain—NO PROBLEM. No problem my ass, he thought. All doubt had now dissipated in Bill; he knew this was a disaster in the making and had a sudden death wish. Nausea began to take over.

My God, he thought, what have I done?

\* \* \*

Hodge had found Sally at poolside and they were making a seamless transition when, with incredible timing, Tina emerged from her suite dressed to kill, strolled around the pool and headed for the parking lot.

Hodge, now on full alert, barked, "Let's go."

Sally admonished him they were not to follow her, but Hodge wasn't buying it.

"This is above and beyond the call of duty," he said, dragging Sally by the arm and following Tina toward the parking lot.

" No, no, no, Hodge" she pleaded. "We're not supposed to follow her."

"Give me the keys," he commanded. He became adamant and she finally relented.

Sally owned one of the most conspicuous cars on the road, a bright red Corvette, possibly the last car you'd pick to remain undetected in tailing someone. That didn't deter Hodge as he powered out of the lot to catch up with Tina. With his adrenalin pump on max, Hodge stayed right on her tail, even as she pulled into the driveway of a magnificent mansion on the slopes of Camelback Mountain.

Tina stepped from her car to peer quizzically at the red 'Vette parked directly behind her in the private driveway, just as John, as in "John Doe," walked from his house to see who had followed his girlfriend into his driveway.

* * *

John stood in our office screaming insults and obscenities at us, all richly deserved. One couldn't help being impressed by his vocabulary. His delivery, too, was exquisite, with difficult phrases such as "...nipple-brained, shit-headed incompetent cock-sucking assholes" just flowing effortlessly from his clenched teeth.

His knowledge of the law was also admirable, citing at least two different grounds for suit every minute for the first 10 minutes. He was surely on the verge of exploding into violence. I was intently focused on his hands, mentally preparing myself to disarm him if he moved to produce a weapon.

Fortunately, he chose legal weapons. Unfortunately, he had quite an arsenal. Within two weeks, we realized we had no choice. To avoid the devastation about to be unleashed on us, we simply closed the doors and walked away.

* * *

# CHAPTER FIVE
## ~ "THEY" Never Really Let Go ~

I really looked forward to getting together with Hunter. In the eighteen months that had passed since we closed down Arizona Confidential, we had occasionally talked on the phone, but had not seen each other in over a year. There had been no issue between us, only the ebb and flow of life that sent us on different paths.

After closing the agency, I had met and become immediately intrigued by a 40ish guy who was just starting a new, national business. Bill Baird was the single-most dynamic individual I would meet in my lifetime. A large athletic figure at 6'1", 225 pounds, blond hair and blue eyes, he had an all-American appearance. He exuded a combination of enthusiasm, confidence and charisma that was overwhelming.

He was from Houston Texas but spoke more like an accomplished thespian—which his wife was—than a genuine Texan. But no matter his accent, or lack thereof, when he spoke, everyone in earshot listened.

He had been an insurance company executive in Houston, where he had become involved in a significant study of the "U-Haul Trailer Rental Company." The incredibly story of U-Haul's success together with the fact that 25% of the USA's population moved each year, convinced Baird to start a new trailer rental entity for an apparent wide open market. His new company, "Universal Trailer Rentals" would be headquartered in Phoenix.

His philosophy of reaching for the stars, pursuing your dreams, was tailor made for me. It's where I lived. He became my mentor, vastly improving my understanding of the art and science of sales.

Bill Baird imparted to me the power of a positive attitude, the importance of goals and many other commonalities of famously successful people. The enormous ground floor potential of this fledgling company did not escape me, and I made a firm commitment to play a role and share in the rewards of its future.

The sacrifices would be huge. Hopefully, this would be my financial bonanza.

My primary responsibility was to develop the dealer network throughout the nation. We targeted every city with a population of 50,000 or more and I hit the road to seek out gas and service stations and other compatible businesses with a storage capacity to facilitate numbers of rental trailers.

No internet existed to identify or locate potential dealers. Over the following eighteen months, I would drive over 150,000 miles, fly another 50,000 miles, and travel every State in the continental United States, if only to pass through. It was not uncommon, particularly in the West, to drive 20 or 30 hours straight from location to location. This before the interstate highway system was born. The Ohio, Pennsylvania and Oklahoma turnpikes were the only freeways in the country.

My trips were from 30 days to as many as 90 days at a time on the road. After a day or two at home, I was gone again.

During that time, I had also assisted Baird in setting up two manufacturers for the trailers, one in Selma California and one in Jonesboro Arkansas. Anytime I was remotely close to those locations, I would hook up three to six open-top trailers, three in a stack, onto my car and deliver them to one or two of my previously contracted dealers. I was anxious to accelerate the viable operation of the system. I did it for the cost of maintaining our household plus all travel expenses. I was convinced the success of the venture would reap the rewards and that was an overriding obsession.

It was an incredible life experience for me, but my wife made the true sacrifices. Judy was left to fend for herself and the kids.

I couldn't really blame her for the affair I discovered she was having during this odyssey, but I could never quite bring myself to forgive her, either. From my perspective I was doing everything possible to secure our financial security. From hers, I was abandoning the family, gallivanting around the country.

In truth, an absolute commitment to ultimate success requires a willingness to pay whatever price is required. Otherwise, it's not an absolute commitment.

Such a path can only be entered with blinders, else one's conscience would irreparably shake the necessary resolve.

The general concept for the business, while not original, was genius. Statistics showed that the average trailer in a rental system would annually produce approximately 100% of its cost.

Investors were sold a trailer or trailers, their investment paying for the manufacture and distribution of the equipment to the dealer, who is responsible for the rental and general maintenance. The company manages and accounts for the activities and revenues. The rental revenues of the equipment are shared approximately 1/3 to the investor, 1/3 to the dealer and 1/3 to the company. And, given the time to develop the system, it works.

Universal Trailer Rentals was going together nicely, and I had completed most of the roadwork. Out of the blue, a small group of investors who had seized on rumors of fraudulent activities and continued to spread the growing tales among themselves became convinced that it was all a ponzi scheme with no actual trailers.

The company was accused of paying investors on phony rentals from the funds of new investors. I had personally supervised the manufacture and delivery of all but about the last 15% of trailers sold, but from their perspective, I was part of the scheme. The District Attorney was brought in, records seized and all business activities halted. The rental centers nationwide were barred from further rentals and issued court orders to hold all equipment The fragile nature of this newly functional operation could not withstand the weight of prolonged inactivity and legal dictates and eventually folded.

Six months after its closing, the State determined that all trailers sold to investors were either in the system or had been ordered from the manufacturers and paid for by the company. Universal Trailers Rentals was issued a posthumous clean bill of health.

It would not be the last time that our system of justice proved itself to indeed be blind.

Hunter, in the meantime, had started a little sales support business of his own. "Appointments, Inc" was an independent phone operation that set appointments for several direct sale operations such as water softener companies, home improvement sales and others. It was a precursor for the "telecommunications" operations that began in earnest some 20 years later.

He had set up office in a complex not far from our prior digs with Arizona Confidential. The core of his operations was the phone room with eight small but equipped stations manned from 10 AM to 9 PM by a staff of highly trained operators.

While I was really looking forward to a reunion with Bill and seeing his office in action, the icing on the cake was that Bill Hodgkins, recently awarded an official drivers license by the State of Arizona, was working for Bill as a gofer, running errands, delivering appointment manifests and the like. It really would be a reunion. And I was sniffing around for a deal.

We spent several hours comparing notes, remembering the agency and laughing over the recollections of some of the wilder cases. We made Hodge part of the reminiscing, but somehow he was different, not his enthusiastic, fun loving self.

Later, Hunter told me Hodge had been much more reserved if not depressed recently. He couldn't seem to recapture the can-do attitude he displayed as our "Junior Partner" months earlier. He was having occasional seizures again, and Hunter feared he was off his medicine.

After several hours, Hunter had to tend to work and I headed home with a promise to return the next day for a cup of coffee and talk of "deals."

* * *

I walked into the office around 2 PM to find Bill in a worrisome mood. He had taken a call from Hodge an hour earlier, his speech so slurred that Bill couldn't make out what he was saying. Assuming Hodge was either entering or exiting a seizure, Bill had instructed Hodge to lie down and call him back when he felt better. He had not called back and Hunter, unable to contact him, was becoming alarmed.

We knew the chef, "Tony," of an upscale restaurant on North Central just a few blocks from Hodge's home. Bill called and found Tony beginning work on the evening's fare. Bill explained our concern for a friend and asked Tony, as a favor to drive over and make sure Hodge was OK. Tony agreed.

The call came less than 15 minutes later. Tony, receiving no response at the door, had walked to a living room window and viewed a man lying face down in the middle of the room, the white carpet soaked with blood around the perimeter of the body.

He was shook. We were stunned. Hodge was dead.

As we were to find later, it wasn't blood on the carpet. In some strange, final twist, Hodge had drunk a quart of iodine. Whatever his reasons for this type of exit, it killed him, the iodine exploding from his body in death.

He had put his financial affairs in order, notes, liens, bankbooks, second mortgages and the like on his dresser. Among them was an IOU Hunter had given him several months earlier for a $1000 loan Hodgkins had made to him. On it was penned, "Forgiven. Thanks for everything."

I wept off and on for two days. There's no predicting where some paths lead.

If only I could understand, before instead of after
What plagues a man to do this thing, choose death in lieu of laughter
If I could know his troubled seas and hear his desperate sound
Then maybe I could shine a light to help him come aground

\* \* \*

His appointment business hadn't produced enough income to justify the 70-hour weeks, and eventually Hunter joined me selling water softeners for Bert DiArmand.

Bert was the best-dressed man I've ever met. His tall, thin frame accommodated his expensive wardrobe with elegance. He was a consummate pro and a world-class closer. "Tall, dark and handsome," fit perfectly.

He was also single, a hypochondriac and convinced that it was a mistake to own more than would fit in his Cadillac, even though he lived in an upscale singles-only apartment. That conviction would enable him to pack up and move with ease anytime it suited him. The only glitch in this strategy was the 90+ dress shirts he owned.

He too lived on the fringe of the real world.

After a few months scratching out a sub-standard income, Bert informed us he had arranged a unique and "very hot" water softener deal in Las Vegas, and offered Bill and I $100 each to move there and sell for him. Ever looking for a winner and feeling our time was up in Phoenix, we decided to make the move, families and all, and establish a new beachhead. It was a mildly successful start to a devastating series of failures.

\* \* \*

The first two people I got to know were classic examples of the futility and devastation of living in Las Vegas with a gambling addiction. Other than their addiction, the only thing they had in common was gender—both were male.

Just after settling into our new apartments, Bill joined me in taking my car to a transmission shop to have a strange noise checked out. Typically, the shop was a small building, housing three bays and a cluttered office.

One bay had a car up on the rack and a mechanic underneath, removing the transmission. We could barely believe our eyes. The "mechanic," a clean-cut chap in his early thirties, was clad in black dress pants, a white silk dress shirt and black patent leather shoes. Arms stretched over his head, he was actually disassembling the transmission while only lacking a necktie and cummerbund to pass as the best man.

"Mechanics sure dress well in Vegas," I said to no one in particular.

He stopped, turned to me and said, "I am no mechanique." The accent was so French it only added to the scene's mental confusion. "But I can do many things."

I'm sure that was a relief to the owner of the car on the rack, because "Frenchy," and that was his name, was now spreading gears, sprockets and other assorted parts on the floor.

We spent the next hour mesmerized by the conversation with Frenchy. He was a former Olympic diver of some renown, as well as a black belt martial arts expert. A handy photo album chronicling an earlier diving career and martial arts background was the immediate answer to our transparent skepticism.

Like millions before him, he had decided to stay in the U.S. and seek his fortune, eventually making his way to Vegas and the anticipated fortune that surely awaited him. He had been stone-broke ever since. Virtually every dime he had or made since arriving was lost at the tables, usually within minutes of receiving it.

This mechanic job was the only work he found that would start immediately and pay him daily, and since he hadn't eaten in two days, he needed money quick. He didn't own any work clothes, so here he was in what he had.

Bill related totally to this straightforward tale of woe from another lost soul inhabiting the fringe of the real world, and invited him to dinner with Bill's family. This began an interesting relationship with a lovable loser.

His plight was reminiscent of the oft told story of the degenerate gambler trying to borrow money from a good friend to get his electricity turned back on so his family could have lights and a stove again. The friend refused, lamenting that the gambler would just lose the money on the tables. The gambler pulls out a huge wad of money, saying, "No, I've got my gambling money. I'm looking for household expenses."

41

In the following months, "Frenchy stories" kept us both entertained and saddened. His gambling came to a head one night at a "21" table in the "Stardust" casino.

Nearing the exhaustion of his bankroll yet again, he had a large wager and was dealt an 11, a "double-down" opportunity to greatly increase his bankroll although it required betting the remainder of his money.

He drew a nine for a total of twenty, a near certain win against the dealers 12, then watched with great anxiety as the dealer calmly turned a 2, an ace, another ace, then a 5 for "21", beating him as if it were so ordained.

Frenchy went berserk, screaming obscenities in both French and English, leapt to his feet, grabbed the table and in one swift motion slammed it upside down onto the casino floor, chips and players flying in all directions. By that time the casino security guards were weighing their options.

They all knew Frenchy since he practically lived there, and they were familiar with his inordinate physical abilities. They knew that in his enraged state any attempt to physically remove him would result in a casino- emptying brawl. Eventually, they were able to talk this smoldering hulk into leaving on his own. In the parking lot, he regained his wits, decided he'd suffered enough with this demon and chose to end it all.

This was just prior to the Howard Hughes era, and the building at Convention Center Drive and Paradise Road that would eventually become the Landmark Hotel was a twenty story empty skeleton, the remains of a bankrupt project.

On this bitter cold winter night, Frenchy made up his mind to drive to this site, climb to the top and hurl himself to a permanent cure in the street below. His state of depression was so heavy he was actually buoyed by the thought of his planned high dive. He pulled his defeated carcass into the cab of his old pick-up truck and turned the key in the ignition. What he heard was the sickening click that signals a dead battery. To add insult to injury, his truck wouldn't start.

He sat, shell-shocked in total frustration realizing that he was a loser even while attempting the ultimate loser's act.

Not long after, he packed his few belongings in his truck, said goodbye, and left town, swearing off gambling forever. We never heard from him again. Chances are he lost his truck at the tables before getting out of Nevada.

\* \* \*

The Hunter apartment was next to ours, and our families by now were very close. Above us, on the second floor, lived Eddy and Nancy and their three kids, also in the same age range as ours.

Theirs was a friendly, easy to like family from Gary Indiana. Eddy was a down to earth, personable fellow who made up for his lack of a formal education with warmth and generosity. The kids quickly fell in love with Eddy, and for some reason, understandable only to children, he became "Eddy Spaghetti meatballs ready." Eddy worked as a superintendent at the nearby elementary school, normally in the evenings and at night after school hours.

Occasionally Eddy would drop off some bags of potato chips or a loaf of bread, explaining it was "surplus" from the school. One day he asked if we would like some butter. When I assured him it would be greatly appreciated, he dropped off a case, twenty-four pounds of butter. I was dumbfounded. We didn't even have room to store 24 pounds of butter. We gave most of it to others.

Shortly after that, he told me he could get prime cuts of meat at 50 % of retail, and if we were interested, to simply provide him with a list of the cuts we'd like and he'd get them for us. We gave him such a list and he delivered later the same day. Since they were all priced, we paid him half of the marked value. But when putting the items away, I realized it all had the local supermarket tags, giving cut, poundage and price.

"Hey Eddy," I cornered him the next day. "How are you getting that meat from Safeway at that price."

"Hell, Bob, I'm stealing it" he said without hesitation.

"You... you're stealing it from the Safeway store?" I stammered.

"I steal all our groceries, as well as meat for a couple friends like yourself, who pay me for my effort. We really need the money".

"How the hell do you get all that stuff out of the store?"

"When you enter the store," he explained, " you're looking at the row of cash registers in front of you, and to your right along the front wall of the store, extending all the way to the far wall on the right, is the magazine rack. Well, I take a few of the paper bags from the store with me, do the shopping, get all the items I want, then, while pushing the cart of groceries around, little by little I bag up the groceries. Then I wheel the cart with the bagged items to the magazine rack, nonchalantly thumb through a few mags, then pick up the bags and walk out."

Well, he was honest about his dishonesty. We remained friends, but I discontinued the "discount buying" from Eddy. But it sure was tempting.

Especially at Christmas time when Eddy offered any toys or soft goods we wanted for pennies on the dollar.

Wal-Mart had not yet begun its reign, but there was a "big box" discount store in town and a good friend of Eddy's from his hometown got a job as a security guard there. As the Christmas shopping heated up, the security personnel were responsible for carrying all lay-away items to a designated storage area. Eddy's friend would carry all such items straight out to his vehicle.

Over a few weeks, he had so much loot that he and Eddy rented a huge mobile home strictly to store the booty. It was an incredible heist of enormous proportions. They sold it all to select friends over the next few months. They were never caught.

Despite all the ill-gotten money, groceries and other goods in addition to his legitimate income, they were always broke.

Eddy loved to gamble.

His wife threatened, begged, cajoled and harassed, all to no avail. His paycheck was gone before he got home on payday. Like Frenchy and all the others before him, he never could accept an unwritten law of gambling: scared money never wins.

Eddy began having serious problems with his teeth and eventually had to have all his upper teeth pulled. Between the dentistry and the false teeth that would be required, he was facing quite a financial hit not covered by his health insurance. So after the teeth were pulled, Eddy borrowed the money from his school credit union. On his way to the dentist to be fitted for the new teeth, he lost all the money in the casino—in a matter of minutes.

A couple weeks later, eviction letter in hand and toothless, Eddy packed up their things and their kids and a seething wife and headed back to Gary Indiana.

Even stealing couldn't keep the demon fed.

\* \* \*

The water softener gig for which we had come to Vegas was truly unique. Bert had made a deal with Larkin Plumbing, a major player in the new-home construction boom taking place at that time. Larkin was doing the plumbing on some 75 % of the subdivisions springing up everywhere. Bert split up the areas between himself, Bill and I. Each of us would monitor our new subdivisions daily, with particular attention to new move-ins.

We wore coveralls with Larkin Plumbing clearly emblazoned on them, and would spend two or three hours each day setting up an appointment or two for that evening when both husband and wife would be at home, to check out the various plumbing and explain the warranties and maintenance required. This would include explaining how to hook up a hose to the water heater and drag it across the carpeted floors out to the yard in order to drain the heater once every month due to the extreme hard water in the area. Frankly, this was a brilliant reality-based ploy. We would then show them a hardness test and explain how a water softener would eliminate the monthly draining, save money, avoid concerns about their plumbing as well as improve their quality of life.

Nearly every appointment resulted in a sale. I was making a reasonable income, but spending several hours during the day canvassing for appointments, then a few hours at night selling, effectively limited my time with my family.

I hired a "canvasser," a young lady to do the daily prospecting and set my appointments, freeing me during the day. This led to my purchase of an 18-foot ski boat, and we began taking family outings to nearby Lake Mead.

That summer was to be the single greatest period I would ever spend with my kids. Skiing, boating, picnics on the beach, playing games in the water and sand became near-daily activities. Although the kids were only 5, 4, and 3, I found a way for them to enjoy the thrill of skiing. I would position them, one at a time, on the thick flotation ski belt I wore, their arms wrapped around my neck and legs around my body, and ski for hours to their squealing delight. It was an idyllic time, much deserved and greatly enjoyed by us all. It was also the calm before the storm.

As the summer drew to a close, so did our sweet water softener deal. Bert had become embroiled in a confrontation with Larkin Plumbing that ended ugly, both parties firing the other. Bert called one day and said simply, "The deal's over. I ended it. Sorry."

Bill and I had been spending time together late at night, after our appointments, toying with two ideas. The first was spinning a miniature roulette wheel thousands of times over a few months and keeping accurate records of each spin. We were having a ball just imagining that we might figure a way to beat the casinos. While we did come up with a reasonable method of winning, in gambling parlance it would be considered a "grind," requiring a sizable bankroll for small returns over extended gambling sessions. Not something we would actually consider doing, but a fun pastime none-the-less.

The second idea we had been kicking around was a viable marketing promotion disclosed to us by Darwin Lawler, a friend of Bill's from Phoenix. In addition to inhabiting a place on the fringe, Darwin had a special place in my mental "catalog of characters." He had done one of the most astounding things I'd ever witnessed.

Months earlier in Phoenix, Bill had introduced me to Darwin who at that time was selling insurance. Since, during that period, I was always looking for a better deal, I inquired about his. He told me it was an easy sale and invited me to go along with him as a "trainee" on an appointment that night. I readily agreed.

As we left in his car that evening for his appointment, he filled me in on the prospect. It was actually two prospects, single women, both employed, sharing a home. Statistically, this is a good "sit" for a salesman.

Inviting us in, she introduced us to her roommate, Linda, and herself, Kathy. Declining Darwin's suggestion that we sit at the kitchen table, she led us into the living room. She and Linda sat on a sofa. Darwin and I sat facing them from two chairs, a coffee table separating us. Both were attractive young women in their mid 20's, Kathy a brunette and Linda a demure blond. There was nothing unusual in the normal small talk warm-up conversation leading to Darwin's presentation. Within several minutes, Darwin laid his loose-leaf type presentation book on the coffee table and began citing statistics and information pertinent to his pitch. Kathy was all ears, leaning forward, elbows on knees, digesting every word. Linda was less engaged although attentive.

Within minutes the presentation became an isolated communication strictly between Darwin and Kathy, their eyes locked as if having a separate, private understanding. Then, some ten minutes into his presentation, he became silent, sitting motionless, his eyes still locked unblinking with Kathy. After 10 or 15 seconds that seemed like 10 minutes, Darwin, now leaning toward Kathy, said in a completely out-of-character coochee-coo type voice, as if speaking to a baby, "I'm goin' gitchoo."

"What?" she asked, her eyebrows furrowed but still locked in eye contact with Darwin.

"I'm goin' gitchoo," he repeated in the same methodical, singsong baby talk.

True to his word, he slowly reached across the table and slid his hand up her dress between her legs. Other than the slight movement of his hand under her dress, all else in the room was motionless. I forced my stare from the obvious to Linda who, like myself, sat, mouth agape, eyes wide in disbelief.

Without another word, they arose, Kathy taking Darwin by the hand and leading him to a bedroom.

Had I witnessed this incredible happening alone, it may have been an entertaining if somewhat shocking event. But I was totally blown away, sitting in silence with a complete stranger of the opposite sex, an all-consuming discomfort enveloping us.

My mind was not in gear and no words of wisdom came to me. After a mind-numbing minute, she managed to speak: "I don't know what to say. I'm mortified."

"Look, I'm…I'm…I'm really sorry," I stammered. "Uh, I'll uh…. just…. uh…. uh…. leave." I made a clumsy retreat to the door, closed it behind me and took refuge in the car.

It took a few minutes to regain my composure and lower my pulse to something approximating normal. Shortly thereafter, Darwin joined me in the car.

His first words were, "I'll write the policy tomorrow."

**Policy?** It was the furthest thing from my mind. After my persistent probing, he explained, " I could see it in her eyes. Its what she was thinking about. She wanted it. Hey, the customer is always right, right? I assumed you would bang the room-mate."

The thought had not even crossed my mind. Now I wondered if that was because of my fidelity to my wife or my shock at the circumstances. What would I have done if Linda had followed Kathy's lead? I told myself I would have remained faithful. But the thought lingered for days. The night's experience was etched into my brain for life.

* * *

To my knowledge, Darwin and his partner, Tom Huey, originated the idea although they may have picked it up elsewhere. Neither Bill nor I had ever seen it before. They called it "The Dinner Of The Month Club." It was a program designed to promote new customers on a regular basis for restaurants.

They had compiled an impressive array of general statistics dealing with restaurant advertising expenses and results, food and labor costs as a percentage of gross revenues and other related information. These industry statistics were compiled into a presentation designed to sell the promotional program to a top restaurant.

The program amounted to a "buy one, get one free" plan with a membership in the "club" entitling the member to one such free dinner each month for a year. One thousand memberships would give positive exposure to a great number of potential customers, getting them acquainted with and accustomed to dining at the host restaurant for a minimal cost.

The promoters were responsible for the sales and retained all sales revenues as their fee. The number of memberships was limited by the host restaurant, usually between five hundred and one thousand. Memberships were sold for $10 through a small phone room operation set up and run by the promoters. Usually, a thousand memberships could be sold in two weeks, netting approximately 50% of revenues after expenses, or some $5000. Again, that was large money in the early 60's, and the program was a winner, benefiting all involved parties.

Bill and I had talked of doing an upgraded form of the dinner club concept for some time and being idled by the closure of the water softener deal led us to make the decision to take a shot at a big payday. We convinced ourselves Vegas was too small for our big plans, and after some minor research, we chose to set up shop in Denver.

Our new twist on the dinner club concept was to create a club with five major restaurants in different neighborhoods around the city, giving club members dining choices as well as five dining opportunities each month. It would also allow us to sell 5000 memberships. We were so confident of its success we decided to move our families to Denver.

We knew it would take several weeks to set up the club and two or three months to sell it out. Money was also a factor. We would have to borrow to fund the project, and couldn't afford to maintain households in both Vegas and Denver. We put our furniture in storage, borrowed money on the cars, packed our personal items in my trailered boat and Bill's U-Haul, loaded up the wives and kids and headed out for Colorado the first week in October.

Just one year earlier we had rolled into Las Vegas with our nation in the midst of the Cuban missile crises. Like most Americans, we had been somewhat anxious about it, but that crisis was resolved without any personal repercussions.

Unfortunately, the crisis awaiting us in Denver would be devastating.

\* \* \*

### ~ Timing Is Everything ~

The first two weeks in Denver were very productive. We had identified and signed up known, highly rated restaurants in Aurora, Englewood, Lakewood and Arvada, communities virtually ringing the city. Our fifth was a well-known downtown eatery. All were enthusiastic about the program, and the various townspeople we spoke to were receptive to the idea, many ordering a membership in advance. Our spirits soared.

It was vital that we pulled this off. The expense of moving, deposits and rent on the modest but furnished apartments we found in Littleton, plus our set-up costs of the first two weeks had all but depleted our bankroll. And we hadn't yet secured a facility for the large phone operation we planed. We found ourselves in the familiar position of ignoring personal debt—rent, car payments etc.—banking on quick returns from the success of the club.

We spent several days trying to line up a room that would provide a comfortable work environment and accommodate 25 phone stations. Oh yeah—and with no money up front.

In the real world, this would probably be considered insane or sheer folly, if not impossible. On the fringe, we considered it a given. It was simply a problem that had to be figured out. And we got lucky.

It's amazing how often luck is the result of pure dedication and the tenacious pursuit of an objective.

Tim Kelly managed a major hotel on highway 87 running through the heart of town. The day we stopped by to meet and chat with him about our club and our office space needs, Ford Motor Company was wrapping up a regional convention in the hotel's convention hall. Tim was a very outgoing and gregarious fellow, a few years older than us. The three of us quickly formed a mutual admiration society.

As we laid out our plans and space requirements, Tim became receptive to the potential and began proposing how we could structure a deal to use the convention space being vacated by Ford in a couple days.

We agreed to pay the hotel $1.00 per membership sold, and sealed the deal with a handshake. Tim even agreed to provide the phones for a minimal daily fee, and banquet tables that would serve as desks for our phone people. We were beginning to believe that "THEY" had finally abandoned us.

A small ad in the local newspaper's daily employment section produced an endless stream of applicants for the phones and within days we were set up in the convention hall to interview and hire. We had hopes of running three four-hour shifts, which would require seventy-five solicitors. Add a couple supervisors for each shift and a few runners to deliver the membership cards and collect the money, and the hiring alone presented a daunting task. Bill and I would be doing the hiring, training, overseeing the supervisors, revising as needed the script we had written for the phone presentations, and managing the overall operation.

It all fell into place quicker than expected. Within days we had fifty solicitors hired and in training and 25 phones installed with makeshift cubicles providing a modicum of quiet in an otherwise noisy environment. We estimated personnel turnover would be high, particularly in the initial stages, as the non-productive solicitors were weeded out. Even then, we anticipated that we could have 15 phones in operation for an average of ten hours each day.

Our previous experience in phone solicitation operations combined with the information supplied us by Darwin led us to expect approximately 150 cards sold per day. This meant we should be able to sell out—5000 memberships— in about 30 days, grossing $50,000. This was an enormous figure, yet totally realistic.

We were beyond excitement. We had followed our rainbow to Denver and now the pot of gold was clearly within reach.

Despite the money pressures on us, we gave ourselves ample time to have our people properly trained and systems in place. We were not going to blow this one. We knew that by beginning our sales efforts that month, November, we would have an entire month to capitalize on the Christmas season.

We set our opening date for Friday, November 23. For scheduling reasons we decided to have one last training and "pump up" session in the morning before kicking off the phone campaign at 11 AM. Everything was in place and everyone was ready. It would be a very merry Christmas.

Except for a few understandably nervous phone people, things began very smooth. A sale here and then there began to create the enthusiasm and excitement that ignites increased production.

Then, as if "THEY" cruelly flipped the switch on cue, all hell broke loose.

Our trained solicitors, all women, were suddenly screaming and crying, some clinging to each other in apparent sobbing despair. One by one, as if engulfed by a rapidly moving brush fire, each leaped to her feet and began babbling incoherently as they received the shocking news over the phones.

President John F. Kennedy had just been shot.

It was bedlam. And within an hour it was over. The room was empty and so were we.

In 1963, television consisted of CBS, NBC and ABC. That was it. For the next four days, television covered the Kennedy assassination. Period. Nothing else. It was known as "Black Weekend." Nielsen's, the television rating service, reported that 93% of America's TV's were being watched.

As the non-stop coverage continued, America sank deeper and deeper in despair, the gloom becoming a cloud that covered our nation. Rather than ease, the tension became heightened on Sunday, the day before the historically unparalleled funeral, when, on national television, the assassin Lee Harvey Oswald was shot by Jack Ruby, a Dallas Texas strip club owner, while in the custody of and surrounded by numerous police officers. It was an indescribably bad time for America.

NBC's Frank McGee prophetically predicted, "… wherever you were, and whatever you might have been doing when you received the word of the death of President Kennedy, that is a moment that will be emblazoned in your memory and you will never forget it … as long as you live."

All who witnessed that horrendous event in American history will testify to the accuracy of his statement. Most certainly, Hunter and I will never forget the time and place we heard it.

America went into a funk and didn't recover for months. It was completely inappropriate to attempt any business over the phone for days, and our efforts to do so proved hopeless. Nearly everything was in a state of limbo.

Everything but the bill collector. Our rent, wages and all other obligations still were unpaid. We were unable to pay the fees and the phones were pulled.

We were back to zero and flat broke. Christmas was less than 3 weeks away.

* * *

Bill got lucky. He found out his parents, still living in his hometown of Roswell, New Mexico, were giving him a business suit for Christmas, and he convinced them instead to send the money. It arrived just in time.

Our eviction notices demanded payment of owed rents or eviction on December 24th. His "Christmas" gift came on the 22nd, and within hours, he had rented a U-Haul, loaded the family and all their belongings and headed out for Roswell to lay low and find some means of subsistence.

Things had worsened by the minute. I was so broke I started siphoning small amounts of gas from cars around the apartment complex at night, to enable me to seek some kind of work.

No one was hiring for anything. Forget the Christmas tree, we were out of food. My daughter, now in kindergarten, told us of her delight in bragging one day during "show and tell" that she had popcorn for breakfast. My kids thought they were having a real treat. Actually, they were having the only food left in the house.

How fortunate that children don't grasp the concept of poverty.

Depression is debilitating, but I found you can force yourself to action. I knew I had to get food, and thought of "Eddie Spaghetti, meatball's ready." I worked up the nerve, visited the supermarket and loaded up two bags. Near the door, I grabbed the bags and, so fraught with anxiety I feared passing out, headed for the exit.

I had taken three steps when the bottom of one bag gave way and the numerous meat products spilled across the floor. I stood, paralyzed, my mind racing between thoughts of running and my instincts urging me to remain calm.

An employee walked up to me with a double bag, muttering "…they should know better than to put all that meat in one single bag." He bagged up the fallen meat, handed me the bag and apologized for the problem. I expressed my immense gratitude and left.

On the way home, visibly shaking, I wondered how one goes about thanking God for helping to get away with stealing.

How can I explain to them there is no Christmas tree?
Can I truly justify such a travesty?
Punish me Lord, if you must, but let me find a way
To shield the children from the hurt on this dark Christmas day.

Tim Kelly was sympathetic with the club's crushing failure, and remained on friendly terms. Somehow sensing the severity of my situation, he invited my family to his home for a traditional Christmas dinner. This magnanimous offer was so timely and so touching, words could not adequately express our appreciation.

For six hours that Christmas evening, we were able to escape the reality that consumed us. The kids, their two and our three, enjoyed each other as well as the bounty of Santa's visit. The food was a blessing beyond our host's knowledge, and the evening seemed a respite granted from above.

It was 11 PM as we drove back to our apartment, the kids having fallen asleep as we left the Kelly's. Judy noticed that Mike, our youngest at three, seemed to be having difficulty breathing. As we arrived home and carried the sleeping kids to their beds, Mike's condition worsened dramatically. He began noticeably struggling to breath.

"My God." Judy suddenly exclaimed, "he's turning blue."

With Debbie and Mark already tucked into bed, we made a dash to the car. Denver's Children's Hospital was only minutes away, and despite the heavy falling snow and icy streets, I sped insanely through the night, Mike now having stopped breathing altogether.

The emergency room staff immediately began working on him with apparent urgency, then wheeled him into the bowels of the sterile building. Within minutes, a doctor gave us grave news: Mike was suffering from a combination of croup and whooping cough, causing the larynx to close; the condition had become prevalent recently in the Denver area, and was extremely serious; that if he made it through the night, he would probably recover quickly; he would keep us informed.

**If he made it through the night?** We were shaken to the core. We paced anxiously awaiting further word. It finally came at 5:30 AM.

It had been nip-and-tuck, but he would survive. We were led to his room where he lay semi-conscious in an oxygen tent. Meanwhile, we were aware that our 4 and 5 year olds were at home alone. We couldn't leave before word of Mike's condition, and simply hoped that the kids would sleep soundly as was their norm. Now assured all was under control, Judy told me to run home and check on the kids, feed them and explain the situation, get a few toys or stuffed animals for Mike and return as soon as possible.

I was greatly relieved to find the kids still in bed. I told them of the night's dilemma, and explained that I had to take some things to Mike, that they would have to watch TV alone for a while. I fixed them some cereal and gathered a few things for Mike.

As I prepared to leave, I glanced out the window across the snow covered lawn to the parking area where I saw a tow-truck parked behind my car, its driver obviously preparing to hook up and tow it. I couldn't believe my eyes or the timing. I knew immediately that the finance company had found me. I was, after all, a "skip." I had borrowed money on the car, then skipped town. Reasons be damned.

I couldn't let it happen. Not there, not then. Impulsively, I ran to my dresser, withdrew the .22 caliber pistol I'd owned for years, and headed for a confrontation. The .22 wasn't exactly heavy artillery, but its six-inch barrel made it somewhat intimidating. I didn't have any ammunition, but he wouldn't know that.

I crunched through the fresh snow to within 15 feet of him, stopped, aimed the pistol unmistakably at his head and said, "I'm sorry, but I can't let you take that car. I'm in a desperate situation and don't have time to explain. Just unhook it now, get in your truck and drive away."

He barely paused in what he was doing, looked up at me for a couple seconds, then continued hooking up his rig as if nothing had happened. I couldn't believe my eyes.

"Goddamn it," I shouted, now clearly cocking the pistol's hammer, "Don't make me shoot you. Step away from the car."

He calmly turned only his head toward me, and said, " Look at the window of my truck."

There, inside the cab with an open window sat a large German Shepard, anxiously awaiting a command. "If I thought you were gonna' shoot me, " he drawled, " I'd have whistled and that dog would have ripped your arm off before you could fire that pea shooter. It woulda' made a terrible scene in this white snow. I figured you'd rather have your arm than your car. "

He finished his job, climbed in the truck and drove off, my car in tow. I slowly sank into the snow on the curb and wept uncontrollably.

I was completely broke, legally ordered to evacuate our apartment two days prior, had a son in the hospital, his mother waiting with him for my return, and now, no car.

My limits were surely being tested. They'd been tested before. I called upon my experiences in Korea when I had doubted my ability to persevere, and realized that I had to keep my wits about me and direct my focus forward, concentrating on where I was going, not where I had been. This was all about survival.

I called Tim Kelly, explaining what had happened in the nine hours since we left their home the previous night. I hated making the call, but had no options. He was understanding and within minutes picked us up, took us to his place, gave me the car, and offered all the comfort he could in assuring the kids would be fine, not to worry. He was my angel. He was my hero. He was a friend indeed.

The Children's hospital had an incredible cost policy. They charged $1.00 per hour of stay. By the following day my bill was approaching $40. As incomprehensible as it now seems, my payment of this sum was unimaginable, and increasing by the hour. Since his recovery was now assured, I decided to take Mike home. Of course, the bill had to be paid before the hospital would release the patient. Since payment was impossible and remaining only exacerbated the problem, I went to his room, scooped him into my arms, apologized to the protesting nurses, and departed.

With the entire family finally at home and Tim's car returned, I sat at the kitchen table, my mind mulling over our pending eviction. Needless to say, I was in a deep funk, although somehow still clinging to sanity.

This was before the age of welfare, food stamps, housing and all the give-away programs then about to be launched by the new President Lyndon Johnson's "War on Poverty." I had no idea where to turn. I had come to a dead end on a one-way street. It couldn't get any worse.

Out of money, out of ideas, out of options and out of luck, I clasped my hands, cast my eyes toward the heavens, and in a sincere plea of desperation, wailed, "Oh Lord, the burden is too great. I can no longer carry it. Not for me, Lord, but for the sake of my family, please give me some relief." My mind was a blank. My brain was AWOL.

Please Lord, end this nightmare. Make it but a dream
Ere I'm lost in madness, locked in a silent scream.

The knock on the door startled me back into reality. My first thought when I opened the door was "The worst just became worse." He had to be a plain-clothes cop. His suit and demeanor just looked the part.

"Are you Bob Radez?" he asked. My futility level hit an all time high.

In complete surrender to it all, I held my hands forward as if for cuffing, and replied, "I am."

"I'm Ben Barris," he said. "I've been looking for you for days."

"You're not a cop?"

"No, no. I'm putting together a small crew for a referral deal down in Albuquerque. Some friends of mine in Phoenix told me you're an exceptional referral guy and a great closer. Said you might be looking for a deal."

I shook hands and led him to a chair at the kitchen table.

" Looking for a deal? Ben, I'm looking for a miracle. Believe me, nothing could make me happier than a deal anywhere right now, but I'm in the worst fix imaginable. Frankly, I'm not sure a whole squadron of angels could pull me from this quagmire."

I laid out all the sordid details of my Denver debacle and thought, just for a moment, that he was about to cry. Or laugh. I wasn't sure which was appropriate myself. Then he told me of his journey to my door.

A referral pitch is one in which the product being sold is secondary to the method of sale—a referral program. In its simplest form, for every person referred by the buyer who will listen to a pitch, a stipulated sum of money is paid for the referral. It's an obvious form of advertising, also called the "advertising pitch," capitalizing on "word of mouth." In a more complex form, more steps of referrals are added. In a three-step program, the buyer is paid for each referral as above, say $10.00 each, then some lesser amount, say $5.00 for each referral from those referred, with yet another step paying for all those referred by the last group.

Because of the geometric progression, significant sums of money can be earned, dwarfing the cost of the product being sold. Ultimately, of course, like many pyramid schemes that followed, the rapidly expanding numbers caused the whole structure to collapse. The late buyer was left with the product, but not huge earnings that induced the purchase. It was legal, but morally questionable. I had become quite proficient with this technique in the Phoenix area, and had apparently gained a reputation as a winner in its fraternity.

Planning a referral program in Albuquerque, Ben decided to shop for a couple of experienced pros in Phoenix, a hotbed of such sales operations since the earlier economic collapse. There, he heard tales of my expertise from some of his old cronies, who told him I had moved to Las Vegas for a water softener deal. Since he would drive through Las Vegas with his wife, on their way to Wyoming to visit his in-laws, he decided to try to find me to complete his new organization.

Checking with those in the softener business, he quickly found out that I had gone to Denver. Incredibly, within an hour after arriving in Denver, visiting with a personal friend who managed a sales organization, he discovered that I had filled out an application for a sales job with his friend a week earlier. It was miraculous.

We spent 2 hours swapping stories and experiences and discovering we had mutual friends. His eventual offer was beyond belief.

He suggested I fly my wife and kids back to Indy to spend a little time with her folks—he would pay the fare. He would be coming back from his in-laws in 4 days, and if I could pack all our stuff in my boat by then—it was parked in the parking lot, full of snow and ice—he would have a hitch put on his car, pick me up on his way back to Albuquerque and tow the boat there as well. He also gave me $500 cash "to take care of things."

To this day, I believe Ben was guided and influenced by a Divine Power. How else could it be explained?

# CHAPTER SIX
## ~ Fantasy Dreams & Borderline Schemes ~

With Denver fading in the rear window, the peace I felt was immeasurable. With the family in secure hands, the pressing debt settled and a new day ahead, the entire load, which had grown day by day over the past three months, was gone. The dramatic change in circumstances was so sudden and all-encompassing it left me euphoric. I was able to relax and slip into a real sleep for the first time in months.

I don't know whether Ben was deeply influenced by my horror story or was just a generous and thoughtful person. But I was truly touched upon our arrival in Albuquerque. Ben delivered me and the boat to a nice furnished apartment, stocked with food, where a rented car for my use waited in the driveway. While I wasn't a big drinker, Ben had learned in our gab sessions that Jack Daniels was my drink of choice, and a fifth of that favorite sat on the kitchen table. He advised me to take a day or two to unwind and rest and gave me directions to the office a half-mile away.

It was a small operation, but impressive. The office contained a staffed phone room for setting appointments, and the goal was to set two appointments every night for each salesman. Given the fickle nature of such appointments, about half cancelled out or simply weren't home at the arranged time. Even so, this provided an average of one presentation each evening.

I usually worked Saturdays and would average 5 or 6 solid appointments per week. We were selling a built-in vacuum system for $599 installed. I quickly established myself as a top closer/producer in the 5 man sales team, averaging 4 sales per week. At $100 commission per sale, I was making a good living from the start, and was able to begin sending money to Judy within two weeks of our separation. Just that quick, life was good.

Our workday started at 5 PM with a rather casual sales meeting, and assigned appointments set for either 6 and 8 PM or 7 and 9PM. I was done by 10 or 11 each night, and fell into a routine of having dinner with one of the other closers, Bill Curtain, around midnight each night.

We would meet at the Fireside Inn, have a drink, exchange results and details of our night's work, and have dinner. Within weeks, we were close buddies, meeting for breakfast and a few games of bumper pool as real world inhabitants were having lunch.

He confided that he had been a contractor in Philly, and was so burned by other's bankruptcies, that he planned his own, hiding significant sums of money along the way. He was laying low with the cash stashed in security deposit boxes to avoid detection.

During the course of our normal bullshit sessions, it became apparent that Curtain had an acute interest in Las Vegas and the gambling scene. He questioned me endlessly about my time there, and, after I mentioned that Hunter and I had uncovered a "system" for the roulette wheel, he was relentless in trying to find out the details. It became a game between us. I would never reveal exactly how it worked, but found a hundred ways to convince him it did. I began to devise a plan for later use.

"Bob, I'm gonna give you a hot tip, as a favor," he said one afternoon. "But you'll owe me one."

"Let me guess," I said, " you want my system in return."

"That's it. How'd you guess?"

"Sorry, you don't have any tips worth that. No way, Jose. Ain't gonna happen."

"Hold on now, you have no idea what I'm offering."

"True, but I know what you're asking."

"Listen to me, wise ass." He was now sounding serious. "You know how, when one of us gets to the Fireside for dinner before the other, we always sit at the bar and have a drink while we wait?"

"Yeah. Happens about every night."

"That's right," he said in a confidential tone, "and who do we chat with that tends bar every night?"

"Beth."

"Good lookin'?" he asked.

"A knockout!" I said. " Playboy centerfold material. And untouchable. Forget about her." Curtain was divorced and, I assumed, horny.

"I have forgotten about her—ever since she told me she had the hots for you, big time, and wants you to know it. Miss Untouchable just became Miss Accessible. And it kills me to tell you this. I figure you owe me."

"Aw, man, you know I'm married. Damn! I wish you would've kept it to yourself. Damn, man, you have no idea. Listen, I haven't had any for months. This is closer to torture than to a hot tip. **Goddammit!** I won't be able to go sit at that bar without getting a hard-on now."

Curtain was enjoying my squirming and moaning. "Hey," he chuckled, "check it out. And no matter what you say, you owe me."

Sex was the mental agenda for the rest of the day. Except for a one-nighter—okay, so it only lasted a minute—before shipping out to Korea, Judy was the only woman I'd ever slept with, and since our marriage, she was never really into it. Like many others of that day, I figured she regarded it as her duty.

To make matters worse, I had never been able to satisfy her, and I had given up trying. That was likely a factor in her affair before we left Arizona. Since our ill-fated move to Colorado, I had been without, simply putting it out of my mind. Well, it was back in.

It was almost 11 PM when I sat down at my normal place at the bar. I was any thing but normal. I wasn't sure whether I was hoping for Curtain to show up or not. I was nervous to the max, laughing inside at myself for feeling so antsy.

I flashed back to my first meaningful kiss. We were 16 and I had been in love with Phyllis since the 5th grade. On her porch we kissed goodnight, our first serious kiss. I would never forget how my knees went weak and I feared I would collapse right there. I was still in love with Phyllis, a secret love that was buried but would never die and never be allowed to surface. Such was fate. Maybe in the next life. But this, this was not about love. This was about sex.

"Hi, Good Lookin' how's your night so far?" There she was, with my JD.

"Pretty good, Beth," I managed. "Got another deal tonight, so the world is good." Tonight I was seeing her through different eyes. She was gorgeous and her body was a solid ten. Could this really be?

"That's wonderful. Why don't we celebrate?" It was an immediate response.

"What do you have in mind?" I bantered jokingly, but really wanting to know where this was going.

"I get off at 1 AM. How about picking me up and we'll go have a night cap somewhere."

"Sounds like a winner," I mumbled, already struggling with a guilty conscience.

I was barely aware of the friendly banter that followed, my mind spinning with both anticipation and guilt. Curtain finally arrived and we moved to a table, providing a needed cool-down. For a while. Five months without sex was a long time for a red blooded all American guy. Still, I couldn't reconcile myself with the idea of an affair. I had come to realize I was fairly unique in my steadfast fidelity, but took pride in it. No, I decided, it'll just be a little female companionship. That's all. My conviction was not supported by my erection.

Shortly after 1 AM she appeared, moving across the room toward me. She was radiant. I swear that I felt the heat as she approached.

She told me of an after-hours joint she liked as we jumped in the car. She realized she was out of cigarettes, and asked me to stop for some. Since we both smoked (everybody did) and I was nearly out, I stopped instead at my apartment, which was on the way, where I had a carton. "I'll be right back," I said.

She jumped from the car too, saying, "I want to see your place."

"Not much to see," I said, "looks kinda like nobody lives there." Without pictures and knick-knacks, a place is just a place. We went in and I motioned her to the couch.

"Give me a minute," I said, heading for the bathroom. When I returned with cigarettes, she was looking at the centerfold in a Playboy that was on the coffee table.

"You like?" she asked.

"Hell yes," I answered.

"What do you like best about her?"

"Well…uh…. to be honest, I guess her tits." I flopped down next to her on the couch.

"Are you a tit man?" There had been a slight pause before her question, and I noticed with growing interest that her breathing was increasingly heavy.

"Yeah, I am a tit man." Now I was beginning to warm up to the game. "I love tits," I said in a half whisper, placing my index finger on the picture and slowly massaging the image.

With that her body stiffened, back arched as she lay back against the couch, moaning softly. I slowly slid my hand into her blouse and under her bra. I was a tit man and this was the Holy Grail.

I had just begun to gently stroke the nipple and areola when her moan became very pronounced, her head snapped back, her eyes rolled back in her head and her body convulsed in violent spasms. And she passed out!

I was motionless, knowing full well she had just had one hell of an orgasm, but no idea what to expect next. This was all new territory for me. Strictly fantasy land. She was out for some 30 seconds, and regained consciousness only slightly cooler than when she had lost it. She grabbed me, clothes were flying around the room, we were clutching and probing and kissing—and we were lost in each other.

Later, we moved from the floor to the bed and went at it again, then again. Each time I entered her and we became lost in passion, she would explode in a gigantic orgasm and pass out. I would pause and wait for her revival, then, already inside her, begin the deep, rhythmic probe again. Within seconds, the guttural moan would precede the rolling eyes and violent spasms of orgasm. It was wild, unrestricted and unlimited sex, like nothing I'd even imagined before. By 6 AM she had surely set a world record for massive orgasms and I was spent. Completely worn out.

"Gotta go," she whispered. "My boyfriend gets home at 7. But I'll see you later."

I was too exhausted to say goodbye, let alone inquire. I was asleep before she was out of the room.

The knock on the door woke me. I didn't want to be awake, but the knock persisted. I reluctantly dragged myself from the bed, wrapped a towel around me, and was surprised to learn it was 11 AM, not that it made me feel any better.

I opened the door and Beth walked in and without a word, took my hand and pulled me into the bedroom. Her clothes were off and I was still standing, blurry eyes and hazy brain, where she had released me, wondering if this were a dream. Without a word, she was on her knees, sucking me into a rigid change of attitude. It was much easier than I would have thought, and within minutes, we were in bed, at it again. It was a 20-minute replay. I could barely breathe. The action was furious, approaching violence, ending in guttural screaming explosion.

"I just couldn't wait," she said minutes later, leaving. "Its the stuff of dreams." And she was gone.

I had been married for seven years and fathered three children, yet felt as if I had just lost my virginity in the past eleven hours. It was much more than sex. It was an education. About women. About myself. About a facet of life that I had thought was only fantasy. And about the freedom and sheer unparalleled pleasure of uninhibited sex.

Indeed, the stuff of dreams.

\* \* \*

"Well?" Curtain asked. He knew I had arranged to take her out.

"I guess bacon and eggs. I'm really hungry."

"I'm not talking about breakfast, asshole, and you know it."

"It was a nice evening," I said. "Is that what you're talking about?"

"Oh no you don't. You're not dodging this one. I wanna hear about it "

"Not much to tell, really. I took her home and we fucked and sucked all night like sex-crazed animals, making love over and over again, totally lost in passion. Other than that, nothing, really. Didn't even go out for a drink, so there's just nothing exciting to tell you about."

He sat silent, mouth open, eyes squinted, staring at me. Finally, "Hey, man, really, what happened?"

"Ask her," I said. "If she wants to talk about it, its OK with me."

"Hey, fuck you. You owe me." There, he had finally gotten to it. I was ready for it.

"Bill, you had nothing to do with Beth and I getting together. But I have been thinking about how we can both profit from my system.

"Bill Hunter and I have spent hundreds of hours logging thousands of spins on the roulette wheel to determine certain patterns. This data gave us a method of play, not really a 'system,' that consistently won, never lost, over nearly ten thousand spins. Practically speaking, it requires a bankroll we don't have. If you're willing to bankroll us on a minimum basis, without knowing the 'method,' we'll go to Vegas and grind it out for 8 or 10 hours a day at minimum bets of $1, for the 10 days or two weeks that it will take to win the bankroll necessary to play for $3 or $4 bets.

"Once we have that, we will have proven the method works and we will have a meaningful bankroll to continue. At that time, we'll return your original bankroll as well as share with you all the data and the method itself for your own use. By starting with minimum bets, we can do it with $2000. We would also expect you to front us $500 for expenses. So your maximum exposure would be $2500. You stand to gain a method of play that, with a $6000 bankroll, can win you $6000 a week. You want in?"

"You expect me to bankroll a system without knowing what it is," he asked incredulously?

"Bill, if you knew, you wouldn't need us. As it is, we need each other. It's a win, win."

The conversation continued for several minutes, ending with an acknowledgment that this "partnership" would be solely dependant on trust. All his. The ball was in his court.

Twenty-four hours later I was on the phone to Hunter. "Bill, you're not gonna believe what I just got on."

Forty-eight hours after that conversation, Hunter and I were on the road to Las Vegas. We were flush with excitement and a bankroll to take a shot once again with a scheme we were confident would work despite never having expected to use it. He had been able to take a two-week leave of absence from his insurance sales, and I arranged a similar time off.

* * *

### ~Winning Is Easy. Quitting When You're Ahead Is the Hard Part.~

The first four days in Vegas increased our confidence level, even though we were asked to leave the New Frontier, the Silver Slipper, and the Stardust casinos. We didn't know if it was because we were winning, albeit slowly, or because our "grind" method was a pain in the ass for the dealers.

It was a mental grind also. We each pulled a five-hour shift daily; about the maximum period we could keep a decent level of concentration. Most of all, it required tremendous patience. The continuous urge over the five-hour grind was to double up the bet to hasten the process. After winning hour after hour, it seemed a safe thing to do, despite risking the bankroll by doing so. We had found in our "research" practice, that every time we deviated from the prescribed betting method, we lost the bankroll. Patience was paramount for success.

By the fifth day, we had almost doubled our bankroll, nearly halfway to our goal. Bill was playing downtown at the Four Queen's. I had just dozed off when Bill returned to the room, only a few breaths short of drowning his sorrow. And he was miserable.

"It finally happened," he moaned. "They beat me. The bankroll is gone. We're out of business." Seemingly returning to form, we had again failed.

With less than a full bankroll, we decided not to push our luck, a commodity that seemed to be always in short supply. When we paid our motel bill and headed back toward Albuquerque the next day, we had $700 left. We decided during the trip to split it between us as compensation for our efforts. To this day, I've never asked Bill if he deviated his betting pattern and lost.

Albuquerque and the surrounding desert were blanketed with several inches of snow when we arrived at 6 AM. I dropped Bill at his car, assuring him I'd face the music with Curtain. Then I navigated the fresh snow on the streets to Curtain's where I brushed the snow from his windshield to leave a message, inviting him to meet me for breakfast at 1 PM that afternoon at our favorite coffee shop. I wasn't looking forward to it.

The look on Curtain's face when he spotted me in the booth was one of sheer joy. That made my task even more difficult. I was in for a big surprise.

With incredible enthusiasm, he shook my hand and effusively told me how happy he was to see me. "Bill," I said dejectedly, "it kills me to tell you this, but we lost your money. Well, not all of it, but most of it. We had $700 left, not enough to play any more, so we split it up and came home. I'm sorry."

I expected a barrage of strong language and worse. "Bob," he was actually chuckling as he said it, "I honestly don't give a shit about the money. I'm so fuckin' glad to see you, it doesn't matter."

"Are you sure you have the right guy," I asked in disbelief?

"Bob, within a day from your departure I started worrying whether you would come back, and by the third day I was beside myself for being such a fool. I just knew I'd been taken for a ride. I've always prided myself with being a good judge of character, and couldn't believe I'd made such a mistake. Now, just knowing you were for real makes me feel so good, the money doesn't matter. I've got more money; trust is in short supply."

I got all choked up, but let him know how much I appreciated him. The feel-good session didn't last long, however, as he let me know our routine was coming to a close. Ben was moving the deal to El Paso Texas. He was starting to get some heat from the city fathers about our sales program. Apparently, one of my customers was at the heart of their concerns.

I had sold a built-in vacuum system to a Mexican-American family of four who lived in a small, austere house, a shanty really, with a dirt floor and no electricity. When I advised them it wouldn't work without electricity, he assured me he could run an extension cord across the dirt road to his cousin's house. Who was I to argue? I'm a salesman. This was a sale.

Ironically, this customer hadn't complained. In fact, they were happy with the unit. But word of the transaction got to the city council, and it rapidly became a consumer issue. Poor immigrant family, no electricity, dirt floors, high-pressure salesman, fly-by-night-outfit—all front page exposure for budding politicians on the city council.

Two days after returning to Albuquerque from Las Vegas, we were in a caravan on the road to El Paso. All except Bill Curtain. He chose to stay in Albuquerque. We would stay in touch for another year or so before losing contact, but I never saw Bill Curtain again.

He told me Beth was in a continual funk over my leaving. I had him assure her it was unplanned, unfortunate, and unforeseen. I'd not seen or spoken to her since our one night of bliss. Hell, I didn't even get to ask her about her boyfriend. I had to believe this guy was heading for his grave prematurely as an emaciated 90-pound smile.

* * *

El Paso made Albuquerque look like a garden. A barren area with barren houses and barren buildings on barren streets. I rented a nice home with what passed for a nice yard in El Paso: barren desert enclosed by a fence. If things went well here, I planned to bring the family out. We had been apart way too long.

With my sales and closing credentials fully established, Ben asked me to accompany and assist him in meeting with our first potential client in El Paso. Ben had gone to great lengths to personally make this appointment, knowing that this prospect could be the difference between success and failure for this venture. We were meeting with the Chief of the El Paso Fire Department.

The presentation went smoothly. I wouldn't say the Chief had larceny in his heart, but we easily found his greed button. Our referral plan required the buyer to provide the names, addresses and phone numbers of his/her friends, relatives, associates or whomever they wished to refer to us. They would also sign a corresponding number of form letters from themselves to the referred party, urging them to agree to see us when we called. The company would mail them and do the follow up.

The Chief recognized immediately that, sent such a letter, no fireman in his department would turn us down. He also realized this $600 purchase would earn him at least $5000 in referrals, primarily because of his position. It was an easy sale, and provided us with an immediate couple hundred referrals that we knew would grant us an appointment.

Ethically, here's the problem: referrals were all time-stamped on receipt, credit being given to the first to submit the name. In the firemen's case, when they bought, they would be counting primarily on all the guys they knew, mostly other firemen, to refer to us. But they had all been previously credited to the Chief. The Chief was at the top of the pyramid, and knew it.

The appointments were being readily set, and the sales began in earnest. I closed a sale on virtually every appointment, usually two each day. The money was rolling in and I decided it was time. I was anxious to be back with my family. I called Judy and explained that I was doing well and things finally appeared to be stable enough for a family environment. She agreed to come out in a few days, right after Easter. I could hardly wait.

In fact, it was a nervous time for referral sales. An "old timer," well known to us, who had a major sales operation in California, had just been indicted on fraud and deceptive practices. Some states and several communities were identifying programs such as ours as "pyramid schemes" and passing laws and ordinances banning them.

There had been no such activity in Texas, so we were not unduly threatened. From a moral perspective, I did feel I was being deceptive, but the bottom line was the customer did receive a good product at a reasonable price. I really was conflicted on the matter. And the money influenced my end judgment. I was tired of being broke.

The family arrived on a Saturday, and I picked them up in my new car. It was a couple years old, but new to me. It was a wonderful reunion. It was great to be with the kids again. The house became a home and Judy was even civil, seemingly willing to go forward. Life was good again. It was a happy time. It lasted four days.

The kids and I were up early, letting Judy sleep in for a change. We were enjoying breakfast when the doorbell rang. All the people I knew in El Paso were still in bed, so I was more than curious. I opened the door to a man in uniform. And a badge. I flashed back to Denver when I thought I was being busted but was being rescued. A sinking feeling in my stomach told me this wasn't about rescue. I was right.

"Are you Robert Radez?"

"Yes I am."

"I'm Sergeant Blair, El Paso police department. I'm here to advise you that at 12 noon today, a police vehicle will be here to escort you to the city limits. You have about five hours to pack your things."

I looked past him for some clue this was a prank, but he looked awfully real. "Are you telling me to leave town?"

"No," he said calmly. "You can stay. But if you do, you'll be in a cell in the El Paso jail by 12:30 this afternoon."

"On what charges?"

"No charges. We just don't want you or your associates doing business in this town, and if you don't leave, you'll wish you had. If you're smart, you'll look at this as an opportunity to travel. Don't be late."

With that, he turned and got into a police car and left.

The kids were all standing at the door asking questions. "Go finish your breakfast," I said as fatherly as I could muster.

"Good God Almighty," I thought. "I've got to go wake Judy and tell her we're being kicked out of town." The phone rang, interrupting my pending blue streak. It was Ben asking if the police had visited me. The bottom line—everybody was packing. Ben knew a guy in Austin that was running a water softener deal, and suggested we go there. I didn't see any options. My tail was already between my legs. Yet another town was in my future.

* * *

I had traveled the entire state of Texas from East to West on several occasions with Universal Trailer Rentals. On the first such occasion I had entered the state from the east near Beaumont at nightfall. It seemed to take forever to finally hit Austin. Before interstates, those 250 miles took 5 to 6 hours. Gassing up before continuing on to El Paso I had inquired how far that was.

The attendant told me, " Seven hunert mahls, and they're all thar." I learned he was right on both counts.

The long stretch of two-lane road through absolute nothingness from El Paso to Austin would have been without a word except for the saving grace of the kids. Judy was so steamed we could have driven with the windows down in January without a heater. It was doubtful she would ever recover.

She was on this trip because she had no choice. It was a miserable trip. The boat, serving as our trailer, made it possible to escape in time. We had frantically thrown into the boat all our clothes and personal items that I had been dragging around the country and, with police escort, had indeed been led to the city limits. We were officially disinvited.

Given a woman, three kids, gas and food stops and other occasional unwelcome delays, the trip took forever. We finally checked into an Austin motel until we could get our bearings. Ben and his wife had decided on the way to Austin that they were going on to his hometown of Oklahoma City. His friend's deal, which drew us to this area, was so flaky I could see the writing on the wall. It was more of the same, going nowhere.

I was staying in a chickenshit motel in a horseshit town with a bullshit deal. That pretty well summed up my life – shit. I'd had enough. It was decision time. Time to look in the mirror and face reality. In one unfinished school year, my daughter had attended kindergarten in Las Vegas, Denver, Indianapolis, El Paso, and now Austin. It was over. I had to find a better way.

* * *

# CHAPTER SEVEN
## ~ Nothing Is Forever ~

We spent three years in Austin. It was a beachhead of sorts. Eventually I became a licensed realtor and established a modicum of stability for the family. As if in the real world, matters other than desperation had meaning. Lyndon Johnson defeated Barry Goldwater to remain as president, and his ranch, minutes from Austin, became the Texas White House, providing my family a unique opportunity to personally see the President en route to the ranch with the entourage that would accompany his every trip.

Less inspiring but no less memorable, my scheduled meeting with a university professor on campus grounds which was violently aborted as the first volley of shots from the Tower at the University of Texas splattered within feet as I exited a coffee shop on the fringe of the campus. I scurried to safety, watching helplessly as Charles Joseph Whitman gunned down 46 others, 13 fatally, from his snipers perch in the tower over the next 90 minutes. I longed for the M1 rifle that I had mastered in the army. "Just give me one shot at the bastard," I thought. But I could only cower in the safety of the building, and watch the carnage.

But I was wrong about Austin. Despite suspecting, upon my arrival, an ongoing, statewide campaign to educate Texans on the use of the word "incredible" instead of "horseshit," I fell in love with Austin, the State of

Texas, and the people. Austin remains one of my all-time favorite cities in America. One of the many events that sold me on the people of Texas gained national attention during our stay there.

A young Texan had been driving his pick-up on the highway between Austin and Dallas with his 10-year-old son. Typical for the "Hill Country" of central Texas, his hunting rifle rested in the gun rack behind him. He could see in the distance a Texas Highway Patrolman (State Police) on the side of the road talking with another driver that had been pulled over. As the Texas father approached, he witnessed a scuffle break out, and as he whizzed by he saw the motorist knock the patrolman to the ground and wrest his revolver from him.

In his rearview mirror he was horrified to see the now gun toting motorist standing over the prone patrolman, the weapon pointed at the patrolman's head. He was already braking the truck to a skidding halt, stopping some 300 yards from the scene. He grabbed his rifle, quickly jumped from the truck, took aim and fired one round, dropping the would-be assailant in his tracks. It was an heroic split second decision to lend aide to a fallen law officer.

Within days, the New York press was screaming for the head of the "barbaric" bumpkin who had the audacity to take the law into his own hands. They labeled the act "murder." They condemned the "cowboy" mentality that seemed willing to condone such wanton disregard of civility. Ironically, some 40 years later, that same press is once again decrying the "cowboy mentality" while ignoring the actual bad guys.

Typically, they never questioned, let alone condemned, the actions of the real culprit who attempted to shoot a cop. Turned out he had already fired one round, miraculously dodged by the patrolman, rolling on the ground.

Within 30 days of the incident, the Governor of Texas, at a special ceremony, awarded the civilian hero a medal for courage and lauded his quick action and steady hand that saved the life of a law officer. It was so logical, so right, that it made me aware of the wrong-headed folly of liberal elitism, which infected the Northeast. It also solidified my respect and admiration of the Texas psyche.

\* \* \*

It struck me as strangely ironic that my father's mother, my grandmother, had died and been buried some 80 miles from Austin exactly 50 years prior. She and my grandfather, both immigrants from Yugoslavia, had settled in

Indianapolis, but her serious illness prompted the advice from a doctor that they seek a dryer climate like Texas. My Dad was 11 when they moved to the Lone Star State, and 12 when she died. They were very poor, and couldn't afford a stone to mark her grave in the Kerrville, Texas cemetery.

Since I was in that general area, my Dad asked that I try to locate the gravesite. Fifty years having expired since the burial in an unmarked grave, it was highly unlikely, but he and his brother and two sisters wanted to put a nice granite marker on the grave if possible.

It was a family outing of significance: the search for the final resting place of my children's great grandmother. The weather couldn't have been scripted better in Hollywood for scouring a century old cemetery, long since filled and unused for years. The sky was dark and angry, providing an endless, irritating drizzle.

It was an impossible mission. Before giving up, I explored the "new" cemetery, an added area through a gated fence a short distance away. In an old superintendent's shack, I found an elderly caretaker, sympathetic to my search. He recalled seeing several old parchment- type records of graves from the old section, and, after a short search, found them in an antique desk in the shack. Armed with these records that amazingly listed her name, we all followed the occasional small, metal tags that identified the gravesites by number. Within minutes, we found it. My grandmother's grave.

I was struck by the unlikelihood of finding her final resting place. In solemn tones, I began to explain the historical significance of this discovery to the kids.

"Imagine, fifty years ago, your Grandpa Frank's mother, your great grandmother, lived and died here, and was buried right here in this spot." I was carefully explaining the event, and believed the kids' seriousness indicated that they were getting it.

Until Mike, then four years old, pointed to the caretaker's old Buick parked under some trees fifty yards away, and asked, "Is that where she parked her car?"

Some things are better left unexplained to the young.

\* \* \*

## ~ Never Ride a Dead Horse into the Ground ~

Despite the welcome run of relative progress in our lives, my relationship with Judy continued to deteriorate. She was a wonderful mother, but it became nearly impossible to live with her. In my mind we were staying together for the sake of the children, but I began to question whether our constant bickering was truly in their best interest. I began to consider the consequences of leaving, but couldn't seriously contemplate doing so in Texas where she had no family or close friends. I didn't want to hurt her, but was convinced we would both be happier apart. Not yet willing to face the unthinkable (divorce had never happened in my family's history and it was a first I wanted to avoid), I reasoned that another change, moving back to Indianapolis among family and old friends, might improve our relationship. In exploring the possibility, I suggested that Judy check on the likelihood of being rehired by TWA in Indy. Doing so, she determined that TWA would hire her as a ticket agent with full credit for her previous employment and with all the standard benefits. She actually became excited about the prospects of moving, the first positive sign I'd seen in her disposition in years. We moved within two weeks.

We leased a beautiful stone, ranch-style home on a large shaded lot on the north side of town, and I began job hunting. Jobs were plentiful; money was not. I was able to scratch out a living selling pianos and organs for several months before being persuaded to attend a one-week "Power of Positive Thinking" course at W. Clement Stone's Combined Insurance Company in Chicago. As a student of the lives of highly successful people, I was already aware of this icon of American business.

W. Clement Stone had borrowed $100 from his mother during the depression, begun selling small accident insurance policies, and had built an empire by the 60's, amassing a personal fortune worth then over $300,000,000. Later, it would exceed a billion dollars. I was eager to learn his priorities and philosophies. While the daily classes were conducted by Stone's dedicated disciples, I was fortunate to spend time personally with Mr. Stone. The experiences of the week would ultimately have dramatic effect on the course of my life.

While not particularly keen on insurance sales, I busied myself contacting small business owners for the company and did eke out a living. However, my sales efforts put me in contact with the disgruntled owner of an appliance store in the small town of Noblesville, Indiana, selling RCA and Whirlpool products. Between his desire to get out of business, and mine to get in, I was ultimately able to negotiate an agreement acceptable to the distributor, the owner and all involved parties. In a most unlikely scenario, I became a legitimate business owner. It was as if I were inching my way toward the real world.

The difficulty of making the business prosper was not my biggest concern. Judy's re-entry into the working world had not improved our relationship, but worsened it. I could see the impact of the advice she received daily from the numerous divorcees with whom she worked and socialized. She became independent to a fault, and developed a constant "fuck you" attitude toward me.

I had already made a commitment to one of the suggestions given at the "Power of Positive Thinking" sessions. On New Year's Eve, I made an honest and realistic self-evaluation, assessing my strengths and weaknesses, determining how to emphasize the former and improve the latter, and setting goals for the New Year. This effort toward self-improvement brought me to realize that neither Judy nor I had been truly happy in some 12 years of marriage. I came to the conclusion that I was fighting a losing battle and violating one of my own tenets, learned at great expense and pain: never ride a dead horse into the ground.

I left my family on New Years day, 1969. I advised Judy that it would be foolish to waste what little we had on separate attorneys, that she could file for divorce, hire an attorney of her choice and have everything except my car. She had one of her own. I would pay child support to the maximum of my ability regardless of dictated guidelines.

With all the heartache and turmoil I'd experienced in my life, the most difficult task I ever faced was telling my kids I was leaving. I explained that I still loved them, would see them often, would always be their Dad and be there for them. God, it was terrible.

Then I loaded my personal things in the car and moved out.

\* \* \*

# CHAPTER EIGHT
## ~ What the Hell
## Happened While I Was Married? ~

I leased a modest apartment in a singles-only complex, although its proximity to my store was the deciding factor. However, I was to find that the "sexual revolution" of the 60's that had gone all but unnoticed during my years of strife, had indeed changed the sexual landscape.

In the '40's and '50's, women were passive in the dating and mating game. It was assumed that "nice" girls were not into sex, but could be persuaded to participate. Even then, it was a mother's duty to caution their daughters that sex was to be tolerated but not really enjoyed. In one decade, these assumptions and conventions, whether true or not, were forever banished from the predominant culture. Women began to openly acknowledge their interest in and enjoyment of sex. After years of an uneasy truce with womanhood, I found myself in a seemingly surreal world of outspoken, aggressive women.

I met Susie through my business. RCA/Whirlpool had their own financing service, and Susie was their agent with whom I spoke on a daily basis. We had hundreds of conversations every month, and a friendly chatter was normal. She was a delightful conversationalist. Even though my experience dictated that sexy phone voices rarely translated into good-looking women, I invited

Susie to dinner. Since her employer forbade such relationships, I was surprised when she accepted.

I was ill prepared for the new world of relationships that had evolved in my absence.

She lived with her parents, where I picked her up. It was a scary moment, standing at her front door. I hadn't done anything like this since I was a kid. I was prepared for the worst, just in case. I knew she was twenty-one, living at home and seemed to jump at the invitation to dinner. Not good signs. I couldn't help but have some grave doubts about this woman, but was confident from our many conversations that I would enjoy her company.

When she appeared in the open door, I was speechless. She was a blond, blue-eyed beauty—the breathtaking sexual beauty of a Marilyn Monroe. This was much more than hoped for. Not only did I have the enjoyable companion that I had looked forward to, but an excitingly gorgeous one to make the evening special.

I had picked a nice restaurant that afforded us an intimate setting. Our dinner conversation would probably be considered "as expected," half get-acquainted chatter, and half double-entendre mating dance. Aggression was never my style with women. Even as a kid I learned that the harder you push, the more resistance you meet. Our verbal dance was enjoyable and safe.

Until she leaned forward and asked, "Would you like to have sex with me?"

What? Did she really say that? I'm sure I stammered a little responding, "Depends on the circumstances." I was serious. I had a track record of jumping at "good deals" that weren't.

"How about no strings attached?" she asked. Good Lord, I thought, where is this going?

"Susie," I replied, my breathing a little constricted, "you're a beautiful woman. Of course I'd love to make love to you. But just like that, with no strings? Are you married? Wanting to live dangerously? What's the deal?"

"I'm not married," she said calmly. "I am engaged. My fiancée is in the army, stationed in Germany. He is deeply religious which has led to him being very inhibited and inexperienced sexually. Frankly, I'm also inexperienced. When we've had sex in the past, it was very uncomfortable for us both. I'm leaving in three months to visit him in Germany and I want to blow his mind sexually. I want to learn everything I can to make that happen. That's the deal. Interested in being my teacher?"

She may have been shocked to learn that I felt as if I'd had only one night of real sex in my life, hardly qualifying me as "Master Instructor." On the other hand, that one night was an education in itself, and I had learned the difference between having "sex", and "mind-blowing sex."

"Ninety days, eh?" I moved to her side of the table, tenderly kissed those irresistible lips, and whispered, "There's much to learn. Maybe we better get started tonight." And what a start it was.

For the next three months she visited me one night each week. We didn't simply have sex. We practiced sex. Every form of sex, every position, technique, and approach that I had ever heard of. We applied ourselves to the subject material. Interestingly, not once were the words "I love you" ever spoken. But the language of sex certainly was. In passionate tones.

My teaching prowess may be questioned, but certainly not her learning ability. She was an incredible student. In truth, I'm not sure who learned the most. She left for Germany grateful and prepared for the task. I had no doubt it would be mind-blowing.

I often thought of the irony of the results of our efforts. Her fiancée would undoubtedly love what she learned, but abhor how she learned it.

Even though I would never hear from Susie again, her influence led to yet another fantasy experience.

I received the call at the store. She introduced herself as Jane, a close friend of Susie's, and said Susie had suggested she call. She too, was twenty-one, and, while enjoying sex, had never had a truly satisfying sexual experience. Before leaving, Susie had told her much of our relationship, and Jane had been thinking of little else since.

At Jane's insistence, I agreed to "entertain" her one evening. She was not a beauty like Susie, but attractive, and with the one attribute that really fired my rockets. She had great boobs.

I was intent on satisfying her, and the tantalizingly extended foreplay was not only immensely enjoyable, but propelled her to explode in a pent up orgasm, reminiscent of Beth in Albuquerque. Her unexpected orgasm seemed to unshackle her, allowing her to freely enter into a sexual state of mind previously unknown to her. A sexual aggressiveness was unleashed that seemed bent on feeding a previously hidden hunger. We were both engulfed in her avalanche of passion.

The experience led me to understand the critical importance of mental attitude in the ultimate enjoyment of sex. I came to realize that a predisposition of "reckless abandon" is the surest route to the pinnacle of sexual fulfillment.

I ended up meeting Jane twice more purely for sex, and began to understand that my greatest sexual thrill stemmed from my partner's pleasure. The sexual revolution of the 60's had engulfed me. It was a good time to be single.

\* \* \*

### ~ "This Is Going to Be Big." ~

It had been several months since I talked to Bill Hunter. We had stayed in touch with a letter now and then. He had moved back to Vegas, and was getting involved in a new concept for selling land as an investment. Known as "Hospitality Room Sales," this sales method is now commonly used throughout the world. This concept was developed in earnest in Las Vegas Nevada as a bold pioneering move by brothers Leonard and Julius (Jack) Rosen.

The Rosens may not have been the first, but were, arguably, the most successful community developers in Florida in the 60's. The Rosen's had piggybacked their success in the mail order cosmetics business into the land development business with the purchase of 1724 acres at Redfish Point, near Fort Meyers Florida in 1957. Their combined marketing expertise coupled with an effective sales organization led ultimately to the successful completion of the community of Cape Coral on that original acreage.

Their marketing consisted primarily of billboards along the Tamiami Trail—the highway from Tampa to Fort Meyers—inviting tourists to stop for free orange juice. Those stopping would be romanced with the tropical Florida lifestyle soon to be available in the new community. But the clincher was the offer to buy into this future bonanza with very little down payment and small monthly payments. Sales boomed.

Other raw acreage was secured in Florida, the Bahamas and Arizona for future communities. Instead of continuing to depend on people coming to the property, the Rosen's gambled on taking the property to the people. They developed a promotional film and plans for "off-site" locations where their home-sites could be sold to large numbers of buyers for investment purposes. Since, at that time in 1969, over 12 million people were visiting Las Vegas Nevada each year, the largest number in a small confined space, it was a marketing natural.

The sales operation was begun in the Thunderbird Hotel, a major hotel on the famous Las Vegas strip. A large meeting room on the second floor above the casino was leased, and twenty-five small tables, each with three chairs were placed in the room. A podium, chalkboard and large pull-down screen in the front and banquet tables in the rear for secretarial duties completed the room. Just as in all the casinos, no windows existed to distract attention from the matter at hand.

Locations were set up along the Las Vegas strip to offer small incentives, such as free cokes, to passers-by to attend a sales presentation at the Thunderbird. Initially, two presentations each day were conducted. Only married couples were invited to attend, and usually ten to 20 couples would show up for the presentations. A sales person was assigned to sit with each couple and elicit necessary information such as name, employment, etc. A designated speaker would welcome the couples, show the promotional/sales film, explain the general concept, then turn the presentation over to the salesman for details and closing the transaction.

Then, as now, tourists to Las Vegas were a representative cross-section of America. But unlike now, Las Vegas was viewed literally as "Sin City", a town owned by the "mob," to be approached with great skepticism and caution. This was the inception of Hospitality Room sales, but making the concept viable would require months of untiring efforts of some very talented people. Bill Hunter was one of those people.

The task at hand was to convince a group of already suspicious people from Iowa and Kansas and Utah and elsewhere, in a windowless room above a casino in Sin City, speaking to a salesman they just met, about a company they never heard of, to pay $400 down on a $4000 contract to buy a piece of land in a place they had never been and had no interest in visiting. And, oh yes, to do it there, on the spot.

Despite a difficulty factor of near impossibility, the concept was a phenomenal attraction for top closers throughout the country for one reason. It was widely acknowledged that 90% of a closer's time was spent prospecting, looking for someone to sell. The universal reaction to this new concept by great closers was, "You mean they bring the prospect to me, and all I have to do is close them?" Some of America's strongest and most experienced closers responded. They had been spending hours knocking doors and making phone calls in order to sell siding and roofing and bibles and vacuums, pots and pans and water softeners. They all hated the door knocking, the "prospecting." They all wanted the opportunity to sit at one of those little tables on the second floor of the Thunderbird Hotel and have prospects brought to them. It was new and exciting and to hell with the difficulty.

As the word got out, a formidable sales organization was developed. By holding a meeting after every presentation, the group was able to compare notes on what worked and what didn't, and the learning curve was accelerated. Successful techniques were formulated. They began writing business.

By the time Bill called, he was managing the sales room. He explained the deal to me, then said, "If you're not making $50,000 a year, you should come out here. This is going to be big." I wasn't making anything close to $50,000, and the thought of moving back to Las Vegas was very appealing, but I had a business of my own to deal with.

Then I had a bit of good luck. An inquiry to my distributor revealed that another dealer had an interest in taking over my dealership. A meeting of the parties quickly produced an agreement, and within two weeks the business changed hands. I had a few bucks, and was free to travel.

# CHAPTER NINE
## ~ Discovering Your Gift? Priceless. ~

After several days of training at the Thunderbird Hotel, I joined Hunter's team in a new location, the Flamingo Hotel, also on the Strip. Like the sales room in the Thunderbird, this was on the second floor above the casino.

In the several months since the Las Vegas operations had begun, their marketing efforts had expanded and improved, and they were able to book five to six parties per day. As a result, the second room in the Flamingo had been opened with Hunter as manager. Optimally, each room would conduct three sales parties each day. The sales had reached a volume of $300,000 per month in each room. Sales parties were generally scheduled for 10 AM, 1 & 4 PM. With three parties each day, volunteers from the sales team delivered the podium presentations. Each room found two or three guys willing, if barely qualified, for this unpaid duty, each believing that they gained prestige by doing so, thereby improving their sales opportunities. Most of these volunteers were boring at best.

In my first few weeks in Hunters team, it became obvious that the one hour spent on the podium presentation and film was largely a waste of time. Most of the sales reps would, upon completion of the formal presentation, turn to their potential clients and say something like, "Disregard all that. Let me explain what this program is about, and how it works." He (there were no she's) would then cover the bases he felt were necessary to close the sale.

Eventually, I complained to Hunter that the reps were having to do the selling before they could do what they were paid to do—close the sale; that a podium speaker had great credibility that was being squandered through amateurism; that the podium speaker should be doing the actual selling and should be interesting and entertaining rather than boring and business-like. We did have a legitimate comparison. Hunter gave the presentation himself on occasion. His dry wit was enjoyable, and he created an impression of professionalism. Although I was still in the learning process, I was closing a few deals and was convinced that we would all do better with a quality podium presentation.

"I agree," Hunter told me. "We don't have one guy in the room that is cut out for public speaking. Why don't you take a shot at it? Any thing you do will look good by comparison."

I had sat through so many bad ones, I already had a good idea of what I thought should be done from the podium. I prided myself as a great storyteller, and had an incredible repertoire of jokes and stories. Some of the top comedians of the day were entertaining in the hotel lounges, available for the price of two drinks. Shecky Green, Don Rickles, Red Fox and others were arming me with an endless supply of great material. The more I considered it, the more confident I became that I could find the right blend of humor and information to give an entertaining yet informative and persuasive presentation. I gave it a shot.

Even though my first podium may have been lacking, it was more effective than most others. I began to give one podium each day, and my comfort level and confidence rose dramatically. So did the business volume of the room. I developed a formula that was garnering the enthusiastic approval of the other reps who were mandated to sit through each podium with their prospective couples. After a brief welcome, I would inquire of the individual couples' home towns. In itself, this was nothing new. However, having driven to every major city in America, and through nearly every other spot on the map while with Universal Trailers, I was able to relate on a personal basis with most couples in the room. This friendly banter put people at ease, and was followed by ten or fifteen minutes of topical or trip related humor, courtesy of some of the best joke writers and comedians in the country. The information portion was also sprinkled with humor, keeping the attention level of the listeners high. Even though I developed a standard routine, I made sure to tell new stories every day for the sake of the reps who showed their appreciation with resounding applause. This would induce everyone in the room to respond accordingly, creating an enjoyable environment for the "show." I got better and better at this newfound talent, and the sales volume soared from monthly totals of around $300,000 to over $1,000,000. Some reps coordinated their days off with mine, to take advantage of my presentations. Others speakers began to emulate my podium pattern, and the company went into an expansion mode, opening three more sales rooms in the next six months.

As the "Hospitality Room" concept became an unqualified winner, other land sales companies began moving into Las Vegas. The expected "standard" for the rooms was $1,000,000 minimum in sales per month. I was still doing the podium "shows" without compensation.

Hunter went to bat for me, but Phil Danti, the Las Vegas regional manager, flatly refused to consider any compensation for podiums. In fact, he stated, "Our program is so strong, we could put a parrot in front of the room to speak and get the same sales volume." Those words would come back to haunt him.

Mr. Danti, as he demanded to be called, was a case study in poor management. If he had any people skills, he kept them well hidden. His arrogant treatment of those in his charge provided on-the- job training of how not to manage people. Nothing is more important to the morale of a sales organization than prompt payment of commissions. In Danti's world, everyone had to assemble in the sales room after the last party on Fridays for the distribution of paychecks. It was not unusual for all to be kept waiting for two hours or more while Danti finished his round of golf.

This boorish treatment by management was tolerated when GAC was the only game in town. As more companies moved in, the best reps began departing for more professional operations. My reputation as the premier speaker in the industry was spreading, and several newly arrived operations approached me with an offer of a paid position as podium speaker. Finally, frustrated with making a significant contribution to the success of Hospitality Sales in general, and GAC in particular, without compensation or even acknowledgment, I accepted a lucrative offer. I explained to Bill Hunter that I had an opportunity to cash in on the genre I had created, and he understood.

I had found a niche that suited me to a tee, and embarked on a road, albeit with a few speed bumps, to great success. I left GAC, but took with me several friendships that would last a lifetime.

* * *

## ~ Good Guys, Bad Guys, Bikes & Babes ~

During the preceding "appliance era" in Indianapolis, I became greatly enamored of riding motorcycles. One of my deliverymen needed to sell a small 100 cc Yamaha, so I bought it from him, more as a favor than anything. But riding it on the streets around the store led to riding it around the apartment complex, and that led to a little larger 175 cc "enduro", made to ride on or off road. I quickly fell in with several other equally inexperienced riders, and soon riding and racing the back roads and fire-trails of Southern Indiana consumed the weekends.

Shortly after arriving in Las Vegas, I graduated to the then new Yamaha 250 cc enduro, then, over the next few years, the 360 yz, an incredible dirt bike, and ultimately a 460 yz. My riding buddies and I honed our skills to near-professional levels, and often found ourselves dueling across the open desert with the top names in motocross racing at that time.

I enjoyed the competition and comradery of others from numerous professions, dicing furiously across miles of an open desert race, later joking and laughing and reliving the experience over a beer and a smoke. And on occasion, going toe to toe with the top riders in the world, happening onto them in the desert, ultimately learning that we were good, but not that good.

The movie "On Any Sunday," released during this period, detailed the serious involvement of celebrities with this growing culture-spanning high-octane participation sport. Steve McQueen was one such high-profile, and very capable participant in many desert events.

I cannot imagine any activity in the world more exciting, more exhilarating, more flat out fun than playing and dicing with a few friends in the deserts of the southwest. Vast open areas provide a wide variety of riding challenges unimaginable until experienced; the Dumont sand dunes thirty miles north of Baker, California, with miles of unsoiled mountains of satiny-smooth sand rising 700 feet into the sky, abruptly falling hundreds of feet into huge bowls, smoothly sculpted by the wind into ever changing form; the miles of uninterrupted dry washes winding their way through the mountain ranges outside of Las Vegas, natural race tracks between the boundaries of dirt and rock walls, leading ultimately to Lake Mead; Glamus Dunes, the 150 mile stretch of unadulterated sand dunes several miles from San Diego along the Mexican border, which attract over 10,000 campers with bikes and dune buggies and four wheeler ATV's on certain holidays; the dry lakes and surrounding cactus guarded desert which dare you to chase the jack rabbits through them with neck snapping 90 and180 degree turns at 50 and 60 mph.

I've done many things for fun and sport, but nothing compares. The high-speed water skiing across Lake Mead at 90 mph behind a hemi-powered rocket boat became tame by comparison. And every black-diamond run down the slopes of Deer Valley and Vail were accompanied by thoughts of how much more fun it would be to do them on the bike. It also provided a great come-on line for the ladies when talking about the thrills of riding: "Wouldn't you like to take a wild ride with a hundred horse power throbbing between your legs?"

I kept my bike (or bikes on occasion) in a buddy's garage since I lived in an apartment with no enclosed parking. My apartment was near the convention center on Desert Inn Road. That stretch of D.I. Road was all apartments. Parking was provided in the rear, off of a wide street-like alley, which allowed access to all the apartments on D.I. Road. A large tract of undeveloped desert lie on the far side of the alley.

The hotels and casinos had three shifts of employees, with the middle shift getting off work generally at one AM. Many female employees lived in this string of apartments along D.I. Road, and came home alone to park in the rear of the buildings, just off the alley. Word began to spread of several attacks on women exiting their cars at night. A large, stark naked black man would suddenly appear and pounce on the unsuspecting women with obvious ill intent. He had successfully dragged one back into the desert where he raped her.

At the time, I was dating a model, Joanie Reynolds, who would occasionally drop by unannounced. I warned her to never come by without my knowledge, so that I could meet her in the parking area. Being a normal woman, those admonitions had the sound of my not wanting to be caught by her with another woman. To make matters worse, because of her public exposure, she had taken, and excelled in, numerous martial arts courses and was confident of her ability to defend herself. I was chauvinistic enough to doubt it, and pleaded that she notify me before dropping in. Which, of course, only strengthened her resolve not to.

One of us would be proven right.

The last time out, my 100 mph YZ began to cough and sputter and wouldn't run over 50 mph. It was left on the trailer with Joe Saligoe's, a close friend, and parked in his garage. Joe was a better mechanic than I and had agreed to help me get it running. Late one afternoon, we both had the time and Joe drove to my place with both bikes so we could tinker and test it in the desert behind the apartments.

We tried the obvious things like changing plugs, then ran it a bit, then tried something else, then ran it a bit. This continued with no success until we had gone some distance from town, hop scotching across the open patches of desert which dotted the city at that time, and eventually worked our way almost to Henderson, some 15 miles across the desert. Realizing it was near dark and not wanting to tempt fate by riding across the desert in the dark, we decided to chance taking the Boulder highway back to Desert Inn Road despite having no license plates or lights, the norm for such dirt racers which are not street legal.

Sputtering along on the crippled bike, I became aware of the siren. I turned to see a motorcycle cop on my tail, red lights and all. Considering my known infractions—no helmet, no light, no tail light, no registration, no wallet with ID or driver's license—I made a snap decision that it would be easier to evade the cop on the big Harley than to solve the legal problems I would receive from him. The desert just off to my right was too appealing, and into the darkness I headed.

Joe had pulled over and I assumed the cop would content himself with one bust. Didn't happen. Riding the crippled bike in the darkness across a desert of cactus, washes, rocks and other unseen obstacles was a damn-fool choice, which got worse. This patch of desert was only one square block, with streets down each side. The cop simply cruised the block toward my direction till I realized I was going nowhere. By then, several patrol cars were assembling at the scene. I must admit I thought it was going to be a fun romp. It wasn't.

I drove to the motorcycle cop who was fuming by then. After numerating my many crimes to my disinterest, he finally got my attention with "...speeding at 70 miles per hour in a 50 mph zone."

"Bullshit!" I said in defiance.

"What did you say?" he fired back.

"Bullshit! This bike won't run 70 mph. In fact, I'll make you a bet. You jump on this bike and if you can make it go 70 mph I'll hand you $100 cash and accept the tickets. And if not, you let me go my way. How about it?"

It only made him madder. He was writing tickets at a faster pace than my bike would run. After the expected sermons, he apparently decided we'd been chided enough and agreed to escort us back to my place to avoid confiscating the bikes. I thanked him through clenched teeth.

Back at the apartment, we loaded the bikes on the trailer, and before leaving, Joe decided to come in for a needed drink. We were hot, sweaty and dirty, and I couldn't wait to jump in the shower. As Joe nursed the last few drops of the icy elixir, I began to strip, anxious to sooth my smoldering anger with a cool shower. I was still cussing the cop, but was really pissed at my own stupid and irrational actions.

Down to my briefs in the bathroom, I heard the blood curdling screams from outside, growing louder and closer by the second. I was barely out of the bathroom when Joanie Reynolds burst through the front door, both knees scraped bloody, scratches on her face, dress torn nearly off and still screaming.

"He jumped me from behind! The bastard is naked. Grabbed me around the neck and dragged me toward the desert."

She was still babbling as Joe and I bolted out the door. I had already armed myself with a Bowie knife that was in my closet, and between my predisposed foul mood and her frightened screaming, I was ready and anxious to use it. The Bowie is an intimidating weapon with a huge, wide 12-inch steel blade in addition to the six-inch wooden trimmed handle. Mine was razor sharp. It had been a gift from a client of Arizona Confidential, and was a prized conversation piece.

As we ran to the parking area, I shouted for Joe to check all the parked cars and I made a beeline for the dark desert area. I figured if he was naked he had to be hiding in a car or in the darkness of the desert behind the building. And I wanted him. I felt I had a license to kill and I intended to use it.

I was completely overcome with a blinding rage I hadn't felt since Korea.

I heard Joe yell that the cars were all empty and I was convinced that the target of my overload adrenalin flow was hiding in the darkness of the desert. The desert landscape was scattered with small Yucca trees and pucker bushes, and I was crashing through them in the dark, screaming as wildly as had Joanie.

"I'm gonna' get you, you son of a bitch. I'm gonna' skin your black ass and cut your dick off before I slit your fuckin' throat." I was a madman plunging loudly through the scrub in the darkness, filling the night with screeching obscenities. All rationality had escaped me.

My mind didn't even process the rapidly increasing visibility as I thrashed about in the brush until suddenly I realized the entire area was brightly lit. I was shocked to the core when my brain finally began to process the stern command on the bullhorn: "YOU IN THE DESERT—COME TOWARD ME WITH YOUR HANDS IN THE AIR."

I looked into the blinding headlights and spotlights illuminating my surroundings and reality came flooding over me. I was a near-naked mad man screaming through the desert in the dark, armed with the largest, most god-awful intimidating knife ever made, surrounded by police who were summoned to get the bad guy. It was a sobering realization.

Wearing only briefs, I had nowhere to hide an eighteen-inch weapon, and knew the sight of it would only exacerbate the danger of my predicament. Not wanting to risk losing this rare, valued memento or my life, I stuck the Bowie in the rear waistband of my skimpy briefs to enable me to comply with the command to raise my hands. As I neared the assembly of lights and shouting police, the weight of the Bowie overcame the waistband, plunging my briefs to the ground, leaving me stark naked, hands held high, the numerous cuts and scratches from crashing through the underbrush oozing blood and collecting sand and dirt, and all under well lighted scrutiny. I expected to be shot, wondering at the moment if I would be dead before the sound of the shot would reach me.

Then I heard a vaguely familiar voice wail, "Oh, my God, not you again!" And making his way to me through the lights came the motorcycle cop who busted me less than an hour earlier. This time, I was relieved to see him.

Eventually, between Joanie, Joe and myself, we were able to satisfactorily explain the situation to the police, and calm returned. The rapist did not, which was a little disappointing. For seven nights afterward, Joe and I traded shifts, lying in the dark on the roof of the apartment building with my 30.06 rifle, looking down on the lighted parking area where the attacks had occurred—hunters, waiting for our quarry. I eventually became convinced that he had indeed been in the desert that night, and he had decided then that this was not a good place to do his bidding.

* * *

Las Vegas was a fabulous place to live in the 70's. The incredible Lake Mead lies 45 minutes to the south with the full array of boating and water sports year round, while Mount Charleston, complete with snow skiing during the winter months and cool mountain air in the scorching summer, was 45 minutes to the north. One of the amazing things about Vegas then was that no matter where you were in the city, you could get anywhere else within 10 minutes. It was the entertainment capital of the world, nearly all available to locals for the price of generous gratuities. And I'm sure it had more gorgeous women per foot than Hollywood. It was said there were more sun-kissed navels around the hotel's pools than in all of California's orange groves.

I was enjoying a moderate, stabilizing success, avoiding debt, supporting the kids and at peace with the world. Making it all the more enjoyable, since I left Judy, she too, was enjoying a successful and satisfying family life. Since she worked for TWA, the kids flew free, and visited me often. After the enormous emotional toll of separation and divorce, it was a major relief to know that both Judy and I were finally realizing happiness in our lives, and the kids had adjusted well to the separation. Although I wasn't getting rich (my long term goal was financial independence) by any stretch of the imagination, I was enjoying a decent lifestyle with a minimum of turmoil.

The unqualified success of the land sales industry brought a flood of land companies into Las Vegas, with 35 separate firms licensed to do business there at one time. It wouldn't be long before the swindlers and fly-by-nighters would ruin the reputation of the entire industry, and turn the State of Nevada against the business as a whole. Until that happened, the competition for talent increased the opportunities for management positions and I, like many of my fellow "pioneers," were replacing the Phil Dantis of the industry.

I had the perfect combination of skills to excel in building new sales organizations. I knew how to sell and close and was a great teacher; I knew how to manage and motivate people, and had personal experience in how not to; I could craft a podium presentation that was dynamic, entertaining and made the closing of sales much easier.

As knowledge of these skills spread, numerous offers came my way. I spent 3 months in Gatlinburg, Tennessee, setting up an off-site sales office for a California company. I enjoyed June, July and August in Minneapolis, Minnesota doing the same, while Vegas baked in 110-degree temperatures. But my first major financial boost came with an opportunity to take over and resuscitate a failing land sales operation in Reno, Nevada and open a new one in Lake Tahoe. It would be the most money I had made to that point which, ironically, led to the worst decision and biggest mistake of my life, as well as the loss of my best friend.

~ A Treasure Lost ~

The overall success of the land business in Las Vegas had certainly started my life on an upward path. Unfortunately, the same time period had proven disastrous to my good friend Bill Hunter. Years earlier, in our days of desperation,

Bill had confided in me his problem with booze, on rare occasion even resulting in a blackout experience. But the problem never seemed to be an issue in his work-a-day world. Perhaps the problem was somewhat regulated at that time by our inability to afford anything in excess. Ironically, his success in the land business led to his downfall. His drinking became painfully obvious, and he went from company to company, burning bridge after bridge. Even though the contrast in the direction of our careers had resulted in a strained relationship, he was no less my friend, and a proven talent in the business.

One of the new land companies to open offices in Las Vegas was the Landex Corporation. It was developing home sites in a small community just off the shores of Lake Mead on the Arizona side of the lake. The developer and owner of Landex, Frank Glindmeier, had contracted Joseph Hollings to create and manage the Las Vegas sales and marketing operations. Hollings and I had worked together, starting our land sales careers with GAC, and had maintained fairly close ties even though we had gone in different directions in the industry.

In short order, the combination of Glindmeier and Hollings led to two sales rooms conducting six to eight sales parties each day, seven days a week. At that point Hollings and I began discussions about my joining Landex to bring a professional podium expertise to the operations. He arranged a meeting between Glindmeier and myself to explore the possibilities. Glindmeier was a down-to-earth but super-sharp guy. He proved from the start to be a cut above other industry execs in comparable positions.

I offered to give daily podiums for a month without compensation to establish a sales production record that could be compared to all other podium's sales records, thereby clearly determining the value of my association. Although Glindmeier was agreeable to the test, he declined my offer to perform without compensation, insisting that I be paid $500 per week during the test period. Yeah, I liked this guy from the git-go.

Ultimately a new position was created, giving me the responsibility of hiring, training, scheduling and managing several professional podium speakers. As a result, I developed a unique position of influence in the management echelon of the company. A combination of my excellent reputation and long-standing good relationship with Hollings quickly led to his confidence in my judgment and my input in most matters. Thus, it was only natural that when the decision was made to open a sales/marketing operation in Reno, I had a voice in the matter, especially on such issues as personnel.

I knew that Bill Hunter had previously opened an office in Reno for the GAC Corporation and had experience and familiarity with the Reno business community. Like myself, Hollings had entered the industry under Hunter's management and prospered from his tutelage. It was no surprise that he agreed with my suggestion that Hunter could be the perfect choice to build and manage the Reno sales operation. With his last couple bridges still smoldering, Hunter was very available. He was introduced to Glindmeier who, with Hollings, finally OK'd Hunter as the Reno General Manager, based largely upon my wholehearted recommendation. I was thrilled that Hunter had an opportunity to right his sinking ship and re-establish himself in the industry.

In the following three months, complaints from our Reno vendors, marketing personnel, and disgruntled sales people about Hunter's drinking and subsequent problems began to mount. Twice in 30 days Glindmeier, besieged by the complaints, ordered Hollings to replace Hunter. In both instances I plead Hunter's case, assuring both Hollings and Glindmeier that the problem was overstated and resolvable. The second instance was particularly intense, with Glindmeier adamant that the Company was suffering irreparable damage in Reno from Hunter's inexcusable drunken escapades. The shouting match in the executive suite didn't enhance my standing with Glindmeier, but won another stay of execution for Hunter. Hollings and I both pleaded with Hunter to clean up his act. But the inevitable came one week later.

The Reno sales office was in the Mapes Office Building, located across Main Street from the Mapes Hotel & Casino. Many of the bookings for our sales presentations came from the Mapes casino, and gifts for attending the presentations were dinners and shows at the hotel. The Mapes was an important cog in our overall Reno operations. Still, the personal phone call to Glindmeier from the General Manager of the Mapes was highly unusual. The purpose was to make certain that Glindmeier personally received the information. Hotel personnel had removed a drunken Hunter from the gutter in front of the hotel at 1 AM that morning, and they were becoming increasingly displeased with our presence in both their hotel and office building.

There would be no attempt at salvation this time. It was over. An enraged Glindmeier made it clear that Hunter would be fired and gone within 48 hours or Hollings and I would be. Further, that he would consider it my responsibility to personally repair the damage as well as re-staff and rebuild the Reno sales organization.

Hollings called Hunter and set an appointment for the following day in Reno, then asked me, as a longtime friend of Hunter's, to accompany him to Reno to soften the blow for Bill. I reluctantly agreed for Hunter's sake and because of the guilt I felt for responsibility in the matter. I was sick with dread the entire flight to Reno.

The meeting was set in a hotel suite at the Mapes to avoid, as much as possible, embarrassment for Hunter. He arrived at the appointed hour, exchanged cursory greetings and sat across from Hollings and I. Hollings wasted no time in the uncomfortable atmosphere. "Bill, I'm going to get right to the point. I have to let you go. The company simply can no longer tolerate your drinking and the resultant erratic behavior. I'm sorry, but your employment is terminated effective immediately."

Hunter sat motionless for a few seconds, his mind undoubtedly swirling with a toxic mix of emotion and desperation, then stood, looking as if he'd just taken a bullet, stared at me as if I'd fired the shot, then turned in silence and walked out. The pall was inescapable. I felt sick to my stomach, but would never have guessed that over twenty years would pass before we would speak again.

Changes of this nature sweep through an organization with the speed of light. Back in the sales and administration offices, within an hour the word was out and the feedback already pouring in. I had to immediately take charge in order to calm the waters. Although every manager has some loyal followers, Hunter's dismissal wasn't disastrous organizationally. But the morale was the worst I had ever encountered. Nearly to a man, the sales reps had nothing good to say about the company. Promised bonuses had not been paid; spiff monies, offered for certain sales or performance, were still owed in many cases, and commission accounting was sloppy at best. The reps had become convinced the company was responsible. By then I had been with the company for several months and knew Glindmeier to be fair and honest beyond the norm. Drastic measures were required. I immediately immersed myself into planning the balancing act of gaining control of the situation without destroying the organization.

In my first general meeting – mandatory of course – I shared my first-hand knowledge of the company and personally guaranteed that all monies due would be paid without delay. I further assured them, in a strong, direct and confident manner that I was a stone winner and within two weeks I would transform the operation into a goldmine for all who worked with me in the conversion. I then fired every person in the organization. When the shock had worn off minutes later I told them I would be conducting interviews in an hour, to give every interested person an opportunity to sell me on why I should hire them back.

Within two days I had rehired all but two of the eighteen reps. In addition I received at least ten applications from others outside the company who had heard of the changes. The drastic move had paid off, and quickly a highly energetic sales force emerged, excited about the future. Unfortunately, I was also receiving information that Hunter, my closest and dearest friend through a decade of desperation and beyond, was convinced I had conspired against him, finally managing to get his job; worse, that I had the gall to attend his firing to gloat over his dismissal. I was devastated. Perhaps it was the intensity of the situation, or my sensitivity to our relationship, or possibly I had subconsciously written him off as a hopeless drunk. Whatever the reason, I made a terrible decision. I concluded that Hunter had unalterably ended our friendship and I decided I had no choice but to write it off as one of life's cruel twists. I would discover years later that after his firing he had waited at home for my call, the expected call from his best friend. It never came. I was an unwitting participant in the destruction of my most meaningful friendship. The loss would haunt me for years.

\* \* \*

When you know how to sell, how to close, how to train, how to structure a wining program and how to motivate and manage, the only missing key to success lies in the marketing—putting prospective clients in front of the reps.

We had contracts with the Mapes Hotel and several other locations around town for our public contact locations, where visitors were offered various gifts for attending our presentations. I began working closely with Bob Loucks, who oversaw the marketing operations. He'd heard of my oratory skills from sources in Las Vegas, and knowing I was giving at least one podium presentation every day to fire up the troops and generate maximum sales volume, Bob sat in for a number of them, amazed at what he saw.

By that time I was truly a master at the perfect blend of humor, information and motivation. My outright theft of some of the best comedy material from the showrooms of Las Vegas coupled with a natural gift for timing, made the 50-minute presentation very entertaining. He witnessed a fairly common occurrence which he'd heard of but disbelieved—couples approaching me afterwards, some who bought, some who didn't, all whom had come for free show tickets or dinner tickets, enthusiastically pronouncing mine the best show in town. It had happened in Vegas, and was happening in Reno.

Loucks, a guy in his forties who drove a very used Chevy convertible with a ragged top, took me aside after a few days.

"If I can get you on the Johnny Carson show, will you let me manage you?" "Sure Bob," I said, "why don't you invite him to a presentation. Maybe we can sell him some land."

People had been complimenting me for some time with such remarks, and while they provide great ego food, I never took them seriously. I was too damn busy making a buck. I had no idea Bob had been a talent agent in Los Angeles for several years.

I was already at work organizing and opening the Tahoe office. The company had agreed with my picks for manager and assistant manager from the talent pool in Las Vegas, but I had a "secret weapon" planned.

Johnny Duncan and I had become close friends since we met in the Flamingo sales room for GAC 2 ½ years earlier. Johnny rarely spoke of his career in the movie industry, downplaying his character roles in some 60 movies with the biggest names in Hollywood. He was a little guy, 5' 4", which led to his natural alliance with other actors of his size like Audi Murphy, Alan Ladd and Bogart. Even though he acted alongside and socialized with the likes of Humphrey Bogart, Alan Ladd, Clark Gable, Marlon Brando and many others, he was best known for, and proudest of, his staring role as "Robin" in the original "Batman and Robin" serial, which shot 15 chapters in 1949 & 1950 for the theaters of America, usually shown on a continuing basis every Saturday.

Because of his flair for drama and the stage, he loved the daily originality of my podiums, often inquiring how I could perform with different dialog each day without a script. I would find out later that he was great with a script, but lost without one. His upbeat personality was great to be around, and we fast became friends.

One year after meeting him, Johnny was diagnosed with lymphoma. He had major surgery, removing many of the muscles of his chest, shoulder and upper arm. Shortly thereafter he was given the bad news—Johnny Duncan, the "Boy Wonder," was given six months to live.

Several days after his release from the "City of Hope" hospital, I went to visit him at his home. He was in the yard, trying to swing a nine iron, still bandaged up and recuperating from the surgery.

Rather than bemoan his situation, I took an irreverent attitude toward his cancer, regaling him with jokes and one-liners about his condition.

"Hey, Fester Chest," I hollered, "you might get lucky and have an improved swing. God knows it couldn't get any worse."

"Fester Chest? Fester Chest? You bastard! You dirty rotten bastard!"

But he couldn't stifle the laugh. He would later say that laugh was the start of his true healing. It somehow struck his funny bone, and every time I'd use it, we'd both double up in laughter.

When he finally was able to attempt a few holes of golf, I demanded that I drive the cart. "I'm not riding with any driver who knows he's dying."

Fortunately, his great sense of humor prevailed, and we both were able to laugh at my continued stream of sick jokes.

"You're the luckiest guy I know. You can smoke all you want and not have to worry about getting cancer."

Referring to his short stature, always a target: "I'll have you cremated, and I'll put your ashes on my mantle … in a shot glass."

One year later, Johnny Duncan was given a clean bill of health with no signs of the cancer. His doctors attributed "Divine intervention." He credits the laughter for "the miracle." We are very close friends.

Johnny had always loved Tahoe, so I invited him to Reno to propose a deal. He would work in the Tahoe office as the company's "Public Relations Director." He would be introduced as such with great fanfare at every sales party, a visiting dignitary, and "encouraged" by the staff to address the group about his Hollywood days and friends. I would provide him a script to follow.

I then taped two hours of conversations with him about Gable, Bogart, Rita Hayworth, his one-time neighbor Bob Hope and others. Later, I methodically selected ten minutes of material to weave into a script of his "off the cuff" remarks. Movie posters and photos of Johnny with major Hollywood stars were strategically placed around the sales room for credibility. Maybe I couldn't find anyone to duplicate my dynamic presentations, but this was a major winner, creating an incredible sales environment.

After the proper introduction, Johnny would spin his tales of the stars, such as he and Lee Marvin secretly violating studio policy by riding motorcycles through the surrounding hills of L.A. and being approached by an unknown, aspiring actor wanting to learn how to ride in order to audition for an upcoming motorcycle movie. Johnny and Lee took him under their wings for some brief riding tips and tricks, and shared in his excitement when he landed the leading role in "The Wild Ones." His name was Marlon Brando, and that role led to Brando's prominence.

After Johnny's entertaining ten minutes, the podium presentation was made, and then Johnny would walk around the room, greeting people personally and shaking hands. Many would ask for his autograph, and he would offer to exchange autographs, theirs being on the sales contract. Many obliged, and Johnny shared in the commissions. The room's sales volume soared, and we had a smash success.

Between Reno and Tahoe, I was putting in endless hours. But I was making over $10,000 per month. This was in 1973, at a time when the average income in the U.S. was $15,000 per year. It was the highest income of my life to that point, and light years removed from just several years prior. And that's when I got the call.

It was midday, midweek, and I was in my office working on some numbers. It was my business practice to take all calls, and this was no exception.

"Hi, this is Bob Radez."

"Hi Bob, this is Pat McCormack. I'm the head writer for the Johnny Carson Show. I also handle many of the show's bookings. How'd you like to be on the Johnny Carson show?"

I was stunned. It took a moment to grasp the question. "Uuhhh …in what capacity" I stammered.

"Tell jokes, sing a song, blow a horn, hell I don't care. I'm told you may be the find of the year. I want to give you the chance to showcase your stuff."

To this day, I can't believe what came out of my mouth.

"Man, I'm so damn busy right now, trying to build a business, I don't think I'd have the time to put together a routine."

"Sorry to hear that," he replied. "If you change your mind, let me know." And he hung up.

That quick, probably the biggest break that would ever be granted in my life had come and gone. I had no number to call if I changed my mind, and Bob Loucks would never speak to me again. I would regret it the rest of my life, and never really understand why I reacted as I did. All my life I had taken incredible risks in futile efforts to get ahead. Here, the holy grail of show business at that time was handed to me and I declined. I suppose, having struggled so long to get into a position of high income, my subconscious resisted the risk of loss.

I have since opined that I'm probably the only person on earth to be invited on the Johnny Carson show and turn it down. What a sheer dumb ass move.

How did it happen? What did I say?
Where did the words come from?
Please call again on another day.
Lest regret leave me empty and numb.

The new managers I had selected for the Reno operation were proving themselves to be more than capable, and I was confident that the office would continue on a successful path. With the Tahoe office on solid footing and the Reno office producing record numbers, the "Northern Nevada Region" was firmly established. The timing was right. October was upon us, and that meant the snow and cold was imminent. I moved back to Las Vegas, again leasing a condo on the sixteenth hole of the Las Vegas Country Club.

\* \* \*

From 1970 through 1975 I was involved in the sale of home sites in communities in Florida, Arizona, Nevada, California and Utah. Each community flourished and the lots proved to be a lucrative investment for the buyers. However, the booming success of the Hospitality Room sales concept also attracted the unscrupulous charlatans. The city of Las Vegas and the State of Nevada became increasingly alarmed that the land sales activities would damage their image and harm tourism. Regulations were adopted putting severe limitations and requirements on the industry statewide. Even the Federal Government became alarmed. Some of the results were downright comical.

The Commerce Department of the Federal Government spent millions running a series of national TV spots warning against investing in worthless property. The spot showed the sun setting over a barren desert landscape, a tumbleweed blowing across the arid scene, and warned against believing the hype of those selling "Sunset City" in the middle of nowhere. Much to their chagrin, they received over 5000 calls from people interested in and requesting more information on Sunset City.

Nevertheless, the anti-land sales efforts of the city and state were relentless, publicly relegating all who were involved as undesirables. Even in success, I found myself, once again, on the fringe of the real world, having visited momentarily, but ultimately evicted.

One by one, the land companies ran up the white flag, folded their tents, and closed shop. Ironically, the only company to withstand the onslaught and remain in business was Preferred Equities, a spin-off from the original Gulf American Corporation by Leonard Rosen, selling property in Pahrump, Nevada. Rosen had been the originator, and became the sole survivor.

But a new industry was taking root with humble beginnings in Florida, adapting the hospitality room sales technique to its product. The southeast Florida coast had a glut of new condominiums, and the market had virtually evaporated. Developers were drowning in unmovable inventory.

One such developer returned from a European trip with an appealing solution to the condo dilemma. He had become aware of a concept that addressed the standard four-week vacations, which were prevalent in several European countries. Twelve friends or family members would collectively buy a vacation house, and divide its use, one month each year for each party. Some enterprising entrepreneur capitalized on that idea by buying several properties and selling separate months of time to individual buyers. Thus, time-sharing of vacation accommodations was born.

Although the original time-share concept introduced in the USA was mildly successful in reducing the glut of condos in Florida, ultimately, it was a disaster, stigmatizing the fledgling industry for years. The developers sold a "right to use" license for their property. When several time-share developers failed and went broke, the bank foreclosed on the property and the "license" was worthless.

Thousands lost money in those original projects, directing national attention to the time-share "scam." Even though the concept was to evolve into several different, safe methods of securing the investment with the actual real estate, the attached stigma made the growth of time-share extremely difficult. That challenge was tailor made for the many recently idled veterans of the land sales rooms. Most saw it as a refreshing change from selling long-term investment to immediate fun in the sun. Unfortunately, many of the same unscrupulous characters that had brought the heat on the land business began opening time-share sales operations.

I was immediately interested when a friend, Jim Freese, called to ask for some advice and aid in putting together a credible program for the Holiday Inns entry into the time share field. Freese was renowned for his closing expertise in the land business, but had little experience in the organizational and business end of a deal. However, he had something of great value.

In an attempt to exert some modicum of control over the burgeoning time-share industry, Las Vegas approved an ordinance requiring a "Time-Share License" to operate in the city. Freese owned a small motel on the Strip near the southern edge of town, and with an eye toward future possibilities, had secured the last time-share license available.

A player out of Lake Tahoe, David Irmer, had begun conversations with Freese. Irmer had negotiated a contract with Kemmons Wilson, the founder and owner of the Holiday Inns chain, to time-share certain Holiday Inn properties. Since no further license approvals were on the city agenda at that time, Irmer propositioned Freese to head up the new organization that would operate under Freese's license.

The venture would be called "Holiday Clubs International," and offer accommodations throughout the US and abroad. I worked with Jim to assemble a management staff, as well as piece together a credible sales presentation. In return, Freese endorsed a proposed plan that I was able to negotiate with Irmer to develop and present the podiums, as well as train others for the task. My only compensation would be $5.00 for each deal written in the Las Vegas operation. Irmer jumped at the offer, sure he was getting me cheap. I was counting on the combination of a credible product, a price of about half that of other time shares, and the talented crew we were assembling, to do a significant volume of business. Having experienced the rapid expansion of the land business, I foresaw similar growth for that venture.

I trained two other speakers, but gave one presentation a day to keep my eye on the game. Within a few weeks, we were generating 15 to 20 deals per day. I was making $600 to $700 per week, giving one 45-minute podium presentation each day, four or five days each week. I was able to schedule my "work" around my golf dates. And it was going to get better, since the overall success of the operation had convinced the company to expand into another two sales locations in Las Vegas.

The phone call came out of the blue, a total surprise. He was calling from Hawaii. His name was Rick Steere, and he ran a small time-share operation on Waikiki Beach on the Island of Oahu. He had spent a great deal of time with a very close friend of mine from Las Vegas, Ron Eckhoff, discussing how to realize the great unmet potential of his project.

Eckhoff readily recognized that the project lacked state-of-the-art sales expertise, and convinced Steere that he had an under-worked gold mine, and that I could lead him to the mother lode. Steere wanted to fly me out for a look and some exploratory conversations.

I had never been to Hawaii, and had long desired to find a deal there. Unfortunately, the timing was all wrong. I explained to Steere that my Holiday Clubs deal was about to become too lucrative to consider leaving. I simply didn't want to take advantage of him, spending a few days in Hawaii on his tab, knowing I couldn't leave my present position. He persisted but I respectfully declined.

Ron Eckhoff and I had started in the land business on the same day back in 1969. He too, had been recently divorced, and was scratching out a new life. We had come up the ladder together. I introduced Ron to dirt bikes, and he was immediately hooked. As in the sales business, he became very good very rapidly, and we made dozens and dozens of trips to dirt bike adventures throughout the southwest. We worked and played together throughout the 70's. Shortly after our indoctrination in the land business, he was promoted to manager of a new room, and later, when I became available, he hired me as his assistant manager against the advice of his boss.

When the land business collapsed, Ron got into land syndication for a local developer, and had gone to Hawaii on related business. By sheer coincidence, he met Rick Steere while there, and the conversation turned to the Waikiki time-share project. As a favor, Ron had toured the project and, recognizing the obvious potential, advised Steere I could provide the missing expertise.

Despite declining Steere's invitation to Hawaii, he continued his attempts to persuade me to change my mind on several occasions. No sooner had he finally given up, than David Irmer informed me that due to the expansion of Holiday Clubs operations, my arrangement with them was too lucrative, and he was reneging on our deal. I would only be paid on the sales production of the original room.

The same day, I contacted Rick Steere and informed him I had changed my mind and would like to see his operation.

* * *

# CHAPTER TEN
## ~ Knowledge Is Power ~

Hawaii is easy to love. Stepping off the plane in Hawaii is akin to an injection of a mind-altering drug. The soft, warm, blossom-scented air, the blue skies and bluer water, endless beaches, a seductively relaxing and laid back atmosphere, all blend into an intoxicating euphoria. The laid-back approach to all things Hawaiian seems only natural.

Rick Steere and his partner/assistant/friend, Jimmy Owens, picked me up at the airport. Both were born and raised in Hawaii, Jimmy an authentic Hawaiian, and Rick a Caucasian who returned after his college education in Southern California. Rick and I were both early 40's, Jimmy a few years younger.

Steere was in charge of the sales and marketing operations of the company, Inter-Hawaiian Leisure, owned and operated by a Japanese/American, Rodney Inaba. Inaba's company was a brokerage for the owner of several floors of condominiums in The Royal Kuhio, a highly praised, state-of-the-art high-rise building just off Waikiki Beach.

Steere's many friends and business contacts from his lifetime residency in the area enabled him to develop an incredible marketing network, capable of booking high quality prospects into the sales room. Although the overall operation was mildly successful, both Steere and Inaba agreed the project had a much greater potential than was being realized. Ron had convinced them, rightfully so, that they lacked the superior levels of expertise that had been developed on the mainland by experienced veterans such as myself.

Steere and Owens not only conducted a thorough tour of the target properties and all facilities for me, but also were straightforward in providing all requested sales and cost data, and all information pertinent to their operation. This information included the heads-up that Rodney Inaba was not particularly fond of "Howlies"—whites from the mainland—and was especially wary of the "…suede shoe hot shots" from Las Vegas. I was both. However, what I saw combined with the information provided convinced me that this project had immense potential, and the more I saw, the more certain I became exactly how to achieve it.

Inaba was most gracious and hospitable in our first meeting, making every attempt to subdue his obvious suspicion of this Las Vegas Howlie. His concerns began to diminish as he became increasingly aware that I knew this business. He invited me to join him, Steere and Owens at a general meeting of the sales force later that day.

There was great anxiety among the 20 sales people at the mandatory meeting. The rumors had spread about the Vegas hot shot who might be foisted upon them. They weren't thrilled. Especially concerned was Rick Wood, the acting sales manager. It made sense that a new guy being brought in on top meant he was in trouble. The mood of the assemblage could be accurately described as "widespread unrest." It was explained that I had not yet agreed to join the company, but talks were ongoing. With that, I was introduced and asked to address the group. It was short and to the point.

"First," I began, "I want to express my appreciation to Mr.'s Inaba, Steere, and Owens for the invitation to visit Hawaii and this project, and to all of you who have been so gracious in welcoming me to your world. This place, this paradise, this island, is new to me. But the business you're in is not. In fact, it is my depth of experience that permits me to say that few, if anyone in this room, have any idea of the financial opportunity this project represents to each of you. Right now, that opportunity is being squandered. Not because of a lack of talent, or lack of effort, or even a lack of desire. As one sales pro to another, I assume those are all in play. No, your income is being limited by your collective lack of knowledge.

"I know there is much concern about this Las Vegas hotshot taking over and telling you how to do things, change things. Things that you are comfortable with; things that are working; things that an outsider wouldn't understand.

Years ago, people were quite happy with the model T Ford. It got them from one place to the other, and they were just fine with that. Today's automotive technology is light years from the model T, but some folks back in the hills of Arkansas and Tennessee are still using a few of them. But given a choice of my new Thunderbird or Mr. Steere's Porsche, most would surely switch.

"Let me simply say, you are woefully behind the systems and techniques which have been developed over the last several years that have dramatically improved efficiency and production, greatly increasing the earnings of those who, like you, work the sales rooms of this industry.

"Knowledge is power, and right now, in this business, I'm the most knowledgeable person in this state. I know how to make this operation soar to the top of the industry. If I join this organization, it will be my mission to share this knowledge with you. Imagine: if, in fact, I do possess this superior knowledge—which I do—just imagine the collective power we would generate as a team when all of us share that knowledge.

"If Mr. Inaba and I come to terms, I will commit myself to dramatically increasing the incomes of ever person in this room. And I won't do it by making demands on you, but rather by proving to you beyond a doubt, that I have a better way before I ask anything of you. However, when I accomplish that, I will expect you to understand that a successful sales force is not a democracy, but a dictatorship. It will be your good fortune to know that I am a benevolent dictator. My demands will be in your best interests, designed to accomplish our mutual goals of success. Toward that end, I look forward to meeting and working with each and every one of you."

After spending a couple days in that incomparable island atmosphere, getting very comfortable with my potential partner, Rick Steere, I knew this was my next deal. I would make it very easy for Rodney Inaba to come to the same conclusion.

I proposed to Inaba that we make an insignificant interim agreement to bring me to the islands. The company would cover my cost of moving myself, my car and personal effects only, and give me a minimal overwrite on sales for a 60 day period. At the end of that time, he would be in a position to evaluate my impact and resulting value to the company. During that period, I would have virtual carte blanc to make or direct changes in any area of the operations, working directly with Rick Steere who would help facilitate my decisions. I believed Rick Steere to be a stand-up guy that I could trust. Even better, I really liked the guy.

My official starting date was January 1, 1978, but I was there by mid-December, settling in and getting a jump-start. The existing sales effort was housed in the Royal Kuhio building. The sales system called for prospective customers to be assembled in a meeting room, welcomed, and assigned a sales rep that conducted a tour of the condos. Each couple was then taken by their rep to one of a series of condos designated as closing rooms for a one-on-one sales pitch. Management was available and could be summoned through an intercom for any help or special circumstances in working out a deal.

Before making the move, talk of my pending Hawaiian deal made the rounds in the Las Vegas time-share world. I received numerous calls from interested sales people. I chose to invite only four. They weren't the strongest people available, but were talented and on the rise. They knew and believed in the systems I intended to use, and, not being "super closers," they also were not prima donnas who might be more trouble than help. I gave them time to get their affairs in order, planning to arrange for transportation and temporary housing when the time was right.

Rick Steere's local knowledge and connections were invaluable in my search for an adequate facility on the beach to house a hospitality room sales operation. We quickly found the perfect location, a large meeting room on the second floor of a beach hotel, with a sprawling lanai (balcony) some ten feet above and expanding out over the stunningly scenic Waikiki Beach with unfettered views of the startlingly blue Pacific Ocean. An airlines group used it for meetings and parties in the evening hours. Since we intended to use it in the daytime, it was a perfect fit. We completed the lease before the end of the year.

We made the necessary adaptations for our use, and it was ready for sales parties by the second week of January. I had already begun working on building and training a sales force independent of the one presently operating in the Royal Kuhio. It was my plan to demonstrate by comparison, a superior system, providing unarguable proof to any non-believers who might otherwise impede the overall success I had envisioned.

I brought in the four Vegas reps as a core to build around. I had also asked for the four lowest producers from the existing "up-list", a roster of reps determining the order in which reps are assigned to customers. The best are assigned first, with those on the bottom having to earn their way up the list.

The sales manager, Rick Wood, a "loveable tyrant," readily agreed, fearing I would demand his best people to use against him. He was elated to "off" his non-producers on me. His production efficiency would likely improve, and mine may be hampered having these "losers," making him look even better. After all, this was plainly going to be a competitive battle. It's the nature of the game and its players. And Wood's team had just set a new monthly sales record of $500,000 in December and was up for it.

Wood worried his job was on the line, but his fire and intensity to win made him a keeper no matter the outcome. The competition would prove to be intense, exciting and profitable. It was an integral part of the plan.

To round out my "new" sales force, I shopped the malls and car dealers, looking for sharp sales people with ambition, eventually hiring a shoe salesman, a men's clothing salesman and two car salesmen. Building around the Las Vegas core with the recently drafted people who were anxious to learn the system, a highly charged positive attitude quickly evolved. With all twelve relishing the "underdog" role, the group bonded and united in the common cause and the atmosphere became electric and exciting. And I had yet to unveil the custom podium sales presentation I had worked on since agreeing to join Inter-Hawaiian Leisure.

We began our sales parties on January 15th with the expected confusion and problems, but still managed to write a couple deals. Each day, as my people became more comfortable and more confident in their roles and abilities, we improved, and the sales volume inched upward. By the end of January, the Wood's team, undoubtedly motivated by the competition, not to mention Wood's infamous rants, had set yet another company sales record of nearly $600,000. But my twelve underdogs, working behind my podiums and using me as a roving closing tool, had produced $400,000 in sales in only half the month. We definitely had everyone's interest.

Perhaps the boastful Las Vegas hotshot wasn't all talk. In any event, the race was on.

By the end of February, Woods was a believer and a partner in the conversion of his team to the new system. While they had maintained their "hot" pace of $600,000 in sales, my collection of "misfits and newbies" hit $900,000. As promised in my introductory address, I had clearly demonstrated a better way, and without making any demands. That I would be able to lead each and every one to a higher income and a brighter future as promised, was suddenly believable.

By April, the sales people willingly and enthusiastically embraced me as "Official Dictator"—memo pads provided by the managers read "Dick Tater"—and Inaba and I had already agreed on terms. Thirty days later, each room had produced over $1,000,000, and, recognizing the dynamics of growth we faced, Inaba, the corporation's CEO, named Steere as President of Inter-Hawaiian Leisure, me as Executive Vice President, and Jimmy Owens as Vice president. With over $2,000,000 in monthly sales, we had become, according to industry figures, the top producing time-share venture in the United States. Inaba treated me with great respect and appreciation, including a membership in the new Honolulu International Country Club. I was very impressed and deeply grateful.

My responsibilities to lead the overall company dictated that I had to install a sales manager in my place, as I could no longer spend all my time in the one sales room wearing the hats of trainer, podium speaker, closer, sales manager and whatever else was required.

I had promised John Faraone the management opportunity before I left Las Vegas. Faraone and I had become good friends in the land business. He too, had been a top gun with GAC, made assistant sales manager with them, later taking over as manager of a sales room. He was the one person Jim Freese and I had immediately agreed should run the Holiday Clubs sales force. When I took a couple of his men for the Hawaii gig, he was a little miffed that I didn't ask him to come. I had explained then that when the time was right, I would give him first option at management. The thought crossed my mind at the time that since David Irmer had reneged on my deal with Holiday Clubs, he probably would try to cut management's overwrites thereby making his managers available to me. Unable to change his stripes, Irmer did exactly that, and Faraone was more than receptive to my invitation.

Faraone was one of the top 3 or 4 strongest closers I ever worked with, and the best manager. I was as thrilled with his coming as he was with the invitation. He brought several of his top people with him, strengthening the already strong room I had built for him.

Rick Wood, in the meantime, wanted no part of being second best, and was working diligently with his team to improve in every area he could with the new system. Since they had all jumped on the new bandwagon, they were on equal footing with any sales organization. I readily recognized the talent on his team, two of whom would qualify for the 10 best list of my career. Eileen Cashmere may have been the best female closer of all time, certainly equal to any male closer and better than all but the best. Adrian P. Howe was the best, and her only equal on the team. He was also an alcoholic of the nth degree in a sales program that served mai tais to our guests three times each day. It was only a matter of time.

Howe, nick-named AP, was British, from London England. His classic accent perfectly fit his pleasant, outgoing personality, making him instantly likable. His rugged good looks were being eroded by the reddish puffiness associated with years of alcohol abuse. Until his words began to slur, he was an enormously charming character. Once the booze took over, he was just another drunk. The latter is why he was fired. The former is why he was rehired. Several times. His exceptional talent and pace-setting sales made it easy for management to be persuaded by his apologies and promises of reform. AP was an ongoing drama.

Eileen Cashmere was a tall, stately middle-aged woman. Her dress, while not quite outlandish, commanded attention, as did her makeup. The pitch-black hair capped the tall, regal bearing and was a perfect contrast to the heavy, bright red lipstick. Eileen relished her role as a caricature of herself. While the first impression of her may have been off-putting, within minutes of her presence, her customers were captured by her class and warmth. Her success served to inspire other female reps to excellence.

The sales rooms were both becoming highly efficient, and the friendly but serious competition was automatic. Steere and I established a lofty goal of twenty weeks of timeshares per day for each room, with cash bonuses for the team that achieved it. This essentially amounted to a sale for every rep on the team. Our overall goal was to hit combined sales of forty weeks in a day.

With increasing frequency, one room would reach the daily goal, but both doing it simultaneously eluded us. We picked a specific day for a major push, declaring a one-day "steak and beans" contest, with the losers being served beans for dinner while the winners dined on steak, along with various cash awards for the winners. The results would take the entire organization to a new plateau of expectation and performance.

Faraone's team set a new team record of 24 weeks sold in one day. Their anticipated celebration was greatly diminished by the Wood's crew setting an even higher record with the sale of 26 weeks. Company-wide, we had established a sales mark heretofore unimaginable in the industry—50 weeks of timeshare sold in a day. We never looked back.

At the celebration dinner, a dejected Faraone, displaying the mind and heart of a champion, declared, "This team will never be second again."

True champions recognize nothing but first place.

\* \* \*

Inaba, Steere, Owens and myself all had significant residuals due eventually from the financed sales contracts, and as the Royal Kuhio inventory wound down, we pledged our residuals in a financing arrangement that allowed us to buy an apartment complex, also on Kuhio St. We had it converted into timeshare condominiums, upgraded the units in a major renovation, and switched our operations to our own new project, the "Kuhio Beach Club."

In the initial planning stages of The Kuhio Beach Club, we entertained the idea of a joint venture with the then very popular international Hawaiian singing star, Don Ho. Inaba's father, a real estate magnate in his own right, was a major player and highly respected member of the Oahu powerful. His family connections were many, and Don Ho was a family friend. Inaba had talked with Ho about the partnership possibilities, theorizing a "Don Ho's Hawaiian Vacation Club." While such a partnership did not materialize, it did get interesting. Ho agreed to attend one of our sales presentations to develop a better feel for our operations. Inaba and Steere both made it clear to me that I was to give that presentation to assure a positive impression. Inaba had emphasized the "fun in the sun" aspects of our business to Ho, and to further that perspective, my presentation began with nearly twenty minutes of the local and related humor that I had developed over time.

Afterward, Ho was most generous in his praise of my work, expressing his surprise at the "theatrical professionalism" of our sales presentation. Steere informed me weeks later, that Ho had approached Inaba for the OK to proposition me on being his opening act in his upcoming show at Caesar's Palace in Las Vegas. Apparently, Inaba squelched the opportunity by explaining that I was too valuable to Inaba, and persuaded Ho to pass on the offer. After my missed opportunity with the Johnny Carson Show, it's unlikely I would have turned down such an offer, had I known.

Despite the success of the Royal Kuhio Club, a significant portion of my earnings were tied up in residuals, and those were pledged in the financing deal on the new Kuhio Beach Club. This would lead to a decision, questionable at best, which would have unexpected and devastating consequences in the future. I decided to gamble with the IRS.

\* \* \*

My two sons were such opposites that had they not so obviously resembled me, I may have doubted the parentage. From his early teens, Mark, the oldest, was totally smitten with the world of sex, drugs, and rock and roll. Against all advice, pleadings and demands to the contrary, he would drop out of high school to pursue a life of perpetual problems. Fortunately, later in life, in his mid twenties, he would face the realities of the real world, repair the errors and omissions of his earlier folly, and become a productive citizen and respectable businessman.

His brother, Mike, was interested in scholastics and sports. Period. He was virtually a straight "A" student, was very disciplined and unimpressed with the denizens of his brother's choosing. To encourage Mike's continuing efforts to excel, I pledged that if he maintained his grades and responsible lifestyle, I would see to it that he could go to the college of his choice. When the time came, he chose Southern Methodist University in Dallas, Texas. I was in Hawaii, committed to making it happen.

Mike's mother was employed by TWA, and I was a "corporate executive," and as "middle class" parents, we were unable to secure significant financial aid. Whether it was our status or our ignorance of the system, we were not poor enough (a recent phenomenon) for help, nor rich enough to afford the cash requirements. I could afford my rather conservative lifestyle. I could afford to help out my former wife, my children's mother. I could afford the $10,000 or so per year necessary to supplement my son's college education as promised. I could afford to pay my $20,000 per year taxes. I could afford any three, but not all four of them.

My commitment to my son was top priority. And I was confident the government would not fail without my help. I researched the potential ramifications of not paying the IRS, and found that filing without paying had more downside than not filing, a simple misdemeanor. Historically, one who didn't file had at least a couple years before the slow moving government discovered the transgression and sought retribution. One needed only file late returns before detection, pay the taxes, penalties and interest, and action was rarely ever taken. Generally, they just want the money—all they can get. I gambled that my residuals would take care of the debt in time, and in the meantime, I was making an "unapproved" loan from the government. Well, it would help get Mike through college. I had honored my commitment to my son. To me, that was immeasurably more important than any commitment to the government. But the delayed price would be steep.

The inordinate success of our time-share resort sales created a migration to the Hawaiian shores of many of the same undesirables that had decimated the land business in Las Vegas. Their marketing methods were aggressive and unwelcome to many who were harassed to attend a presentation. The beaches were flooded with agents hitting on any and everybody in sight. The city, county and state officials grew increasingly concerned the image problem until finally time-share became an unwelcome entity in the state. The official turn-off was especially keen in Waikiki Beach.

Once again, I found myself in a socially condemned enterprise, pushed further and further out onto the fringe of the real world.

Rick Wood and I had become close friends and golf buddies, and shared a passion for a new entertainment phenomenon that had taken Japan by storm. With the dominant Japanese influence in Hawaii, it was also sweeping the islands. Stand-up electronic video games were becoming the rage, appearing in huge emporiums around Honolulu. American manufacturers such as Atari were starting to make inroads in the fledgling business with "Asteroids" and other entries, but the video emporium onslaught had not really begun on the mainland.

As the Kuhio Beach Club was in its final sales phase, Rick and I had our antenna up for future deals of interest. Because of our insatiable appetite for playing the video games, we began looking at the facts and figures relating to the business side of the games. We liked what we found and when the Beach Club was sold out, we busied ourselves with the plans for a new venture on the mainland.

Rick's parents lived just outside of Phoenix, Arizona in the town of Litchfield Park. He was originally from Ohio, but became an Arizonan when his father took over the highly technical Goodyear plant in Litchfield Park. Rick's alma mater was Arizona State University. We both loved the area, were very familiar with it, and were well aware of its dynamic growth. Like most major cities at the time, the only video game businesses were small arcades in a few malls. To our knowledge, no one had considered an emporium on the scale we envisioned. We moved to Tempe, a suburb of Phoenix and home of ASU.

Before leaving Hawaii, we hooked up with a third partner, Ron Mercer. Ron and I had known each other for years, dating back to Indiana. He was an entrepreneurial guy who had the Midas touch. Virtually everything he became involved with worked out well. Ron had been a silent partner of mine in the appliance business in Indiana. He had since moved to Hawaii and was involved in real estate there.

Ron loved the space-age themed concept Rick and I were developing and wanted to get involved. We could use the additional capital, but he would also play a vital and active role in the operation. His major responsibility entailed the acquisition of the games.

As Wood and I worked on creating the "Starship Fantasy" concept—the unanimous choice of some 30 names we considered—Ron was contacting manufacturers and distributors of the games, preparing the orders and methods of sale or lease on the numbers and types of games specified by Wood and I. These were integral details relative to the final configuration of the store. Together we formed "The Razwood Corporation," combining my nickname with Rick's last name.

We found an ideal location between several high schools and in close proximity to the University. It was a freestanding building on the fringe of a shopping center property, with 6000 square feet of usable space. Since this was a pioneering effort with "pin-ball arcade" inference, negotiating the lease with the Center was a near impossible task, but we finally convinced the decision makers that this would be a virtually antiseptic operation. We were in.

The original "Star Wars" movie had only been out for several months and was a blockbuster of unprecedented proportions. Simultaneously, the TV series "Star Trek" was at its peak. We contracted an architect to design the interior of our building in the image of the control room and other futuristic areas of the "Enterprise," the star ship featured on "Star Trek."

The 15-foot high ceilings were darkened, and provided a perfect space-like background for the three-foot to five-foot model space ships that had been built for us, resembling various space vehicles from "Star Wars." These were strategically installed and well lit in the black space above the game floor, and appeared to be floating in space. The entrance to the building was through a kaleidoscopic tunnel leading into the (earthbound) "Starship Fantasy," our new emporium, with some 200 state-of-the-art electronic video games.

"Interior of 'The Starship Fantasy'"

Our attendants, dressed in Star Trek- like uniforms, would sell tokens for the games, give advice and tips on how to play, and give the occasional free game as a learning experience to a newcomer. No smoking or drinking was allowed on the premises, and a legitimate uniformed guard was always present to insure the security of all patrons. Any one who was ejected for unacceptable behavior was first photographed with a Polaroid camera, and their picture was immediately posted on a "not welcome" bulletin board. It was a bold execution of a brilliant scheme. And it worked big time. Nearly overnight, the "Starship" became the "in" spot.

Within two weeks the word had spread and we had a packed house nearly every night. On weekend evenings, lines formed into the parking lot, with hundreds waiting to be let in. The fire Marshal was a weekly visitor with an eye toward our legal "capacity" of 350. Parents started stopping by to check out the attraction that had become the new hangout, the only one at which kids from competing schools would mingle together in an enjoyable environment without problems.

# Close-ups

THE ARIZONA REPUBLIC
Thursday, February 5, 1981

## SPACED OUT

" You're floating freely in space. You fly the ship and do combat with flying saucers trying to annihilate you. The better you get, the longer you can play for a quarter "

Bob Radez, left, and Rick Wood have built a fantasy of video electronic games in Tempe.

## Developers cook up feast of electronic games

By Gail Tabor
Republic Staff

A "little portfolio of dreams" has turned into reality for three Honolulu-cum-Phoenix businessmen. And they say there isn't another one like it in the world.

Starship Fantasy, a video electronic family entertainment center in Tempe, is the realization of many months of developing that portfolio.

With lights flashing and spinning and 150 machines waiting for players, the center and its outer-space-garbed attendants blasted off into fun galaxy with its opening last week, after a month's "shakedown cruise."

Rick Wood, Bob Radez and Ron Mercer are president, vice president and secretary-treasurer of the corporation that owns the center. They are aiming for family trade and stress safety and service in going after it.

With other arcades and game centers packing in the crowds, it seems legitimate to ask the owners, "What's different about yours?"

"You could ask the difference between hamburger and steak," Radez shoots back indignantly. "They're arcades with a lot of games. We're in the video entertainment business."

The men contend that arcades (they pronounce the word with a diedainful sniff) contain lots of kids, a dirty and sometimes scruffy linoleum floor, spilled drinks, pinball machines mixed in with electronic games, a machine on the wall to give change, and a potential for rowdyism that gives many parents acute heartburn.

Rowdyism wasn't part of their portfolio, and the owners say the only thing Starship has in common with arcades is "lots of kids." There's a cashier to make change. Uniformed attendants provide assistance and security. They do not allow smoking, drinking, gum or tobacco chewing, or consumption of food or beverages at any time.

"When you open a place like this, kids are going to try you," explains Radez. "But once we laid down the law, after three or four weeks the kids were taking lots of pride in 'their' place, and there's peer pressure (to behave). We've made it clear we want them to enjoy it, but they're in our home and they conduct themselves accordingly."

Wood says, "With (this behavior) and by being clean, plush and comfortable, we attract families. And teen-agers can come and meet socially. It's not a bar. It's an atmosphere they can consider their own."

The number of adults anxious to enter a teen-ager's bailiwick could be open to debate, but Wood maintains the two generations meet comfortably while zapping alien invaders into microsmithereens.

He relates the story of a man who came in regularly with his teen-age son, then showed up alone. When Wood inquired about the offspring, the father replied:

"He's at home. You know, I taught him softball, I taught him football, I help him with his math. But he kills me at this game, and I'm here to practice."

Practice is the key to gaining expertise on the sophisticated games, and many people are discovering the fun factor is not limited to any age group.

"They require tremendous skill, and it's a challenge," notes Wood.

Asteroids is one of the most popular games. Esquire magazine devoted several pages of its February issue to the national Asteroids mania that turns grown men into fanatics. Wall Street brokers and bankers join sneakered students in fighting quarters as fast as the machine can take them.

According to Radez, in Asteroids the player has total control over his destiny. "You're floating freely in space," he says. "You fly the ship and do combat with flying saucers trying to annihilate you. The better you get, the longer you can play for a quarter."

Battle Zone, a three-dimensional game, also is popular, and Wood says kids line up to take their turn on an alien surface battling enemy tanks on a radar screen.

Electronic video games may be reaching a peak on the mainland, but in Honolulu, where the three owners were in real estate and resort development, the craze started earlier.

"Hawaii has close ties to Japan, where many of the machines and boards are made," explains Radez. "There was a tremendous influx of games into Honolulu, and they were accepted two to five years before catching on (here)."

Radez and Wood started playing the games for enjoyment, got involved as an investment, then decided the country was ready for an alternate form of entertainment that didn't take a bundle of money and gallons of gas.

"We said, 'Let's do this thing and do it right, in a way that will impress even the most cynical of people who would think it's just another arcade,'" Radez recalls.

Because of their Honolulu connection, the men claim they have games that aren't found anywhere else in the Valley and that new ones will be brought in every three or four months.

Expansion plans for the company are concentrated in the Sun Belt, and Phoenix probably will be used as a base of operations.

For Wood and Radez, it's not completely unfamiliar territory. Wood's parents are Mr. and Mrs. Wayne Wood (he's general manager of Goodyear's Aerospace Division) and the family moved here in 1966. He graduated from Arizona State University where he "played a little football."

Radez moved to Phoenix from Indiana in 1959, before "the boom" started, and lived here three years.

"People appreciated (Phoenix) then," he says, adding that not a day went by that someone didn't express happiness at living here rather than complaining about this or that.

"I'm disappointed they don't still feel what a great place this is," he said.

"Making the News – Arizona Republic"

Eventually, we tapped the adult market separately by staying open "after hours," midnight till two or three in the morning, for the 21 and over crowd. Articles on our sensational success started appearing in the local papers as well as on at least one national major network telecast. A multi-million dollar offer

112

came from a group in Texas for rights to build Starship Fantasys throughout Texas. The group's proposal guaranteed to open a significant number of Starships each year for a five-year period and buy or lease all equipment through us. It was a multi-million dollar proposal. We directed our attorneys to draft the appropriate documents and do the necessary groundwork for franchising the system throughout the nation. We had arrived. But we had also attracted some worried attention.

The Midway Manufacturing Co., manufacturer of "Bally" machines, also had designs on the video game industry. They were manufacturing games as well as opening small arcades in the shopping malls of major cities throughout the nation, using their own games.

The enormous popularity of our concept with obvious national implications must have caused competitive concerns about their national plans and commitments. Their legal department sent us a letter demanding we cease and desist our business, accusing us of using illegal machines. Bally's is a major player in the gaming industry, a leading manufacturer of slot machines and other gaming devices, as well as developer/owners of hotel/casinos bearing its name. I had spent years as a resident in Las Vegas and knew the power and willingness of the gaming lords to accomplish their goals. Their threats were to be taken seriously.

We huddled with Ron to double-check our machine contracts and related documentation, all of which had specific clauses guaranteeing the legality of all our equipment.

We drafted a letter to Midway, surmising there existed some misunderstanding regarding our machines. Further, that our expansion plans called for the purchase and use of thousands of their machines and we wished to resolve any concerns they might have regarding our business. We proposed, as the chief executives of our company, to visit their headquarters in Chicago, sit down with their decision makers and discuss their concerns. A follow up phone call resulted in a scheduled meeting with their President and the Chief Operating Officer.

In Chicago, Wood and I were led into a conference room full of attorneys. A couple company execs rounded out the apparent lynch mob. We had come to resolve any concerns through a candid discussion with our counterparts at Midway. Although the meeting was arranged on that basis, it was immediately apparent that only Rick and I sought resolution.

Several times in the past I had experienced the intimidation of being deposed as a witness for various legal matters. This was a deposition, not a meeting. The attorneys were like sharks in a feeding frenzy, ecstatic over the opportunity to find any information that could be used to damage us. It was obvious from the opening salvo that they were out to stop us, and nothing we could say or do would change their course of action. We were able to learn that they had persuaded the feds that any machines that were manufactured in Japan were "knock-offs" and thus illegal. Neither our contracts to the contrary or our intentions to remedy any problems had any effect on the outcome of the "meeting."

Heading back to Tempe, we felt as though we had just escaped with a warning shot fired across our bow, and that the dark forces had made their intentions clear.

"Did we just witness the mob in business camouflage?" Wood asked.

"I guess the feeling is unmistakable," I said. "I couldn't help but think we were in the back room of a casino, about to be worked over for cheating."

"I'd be willing to bet some of those 'attorneys' were carrying switch blade knives," Wood mused, only half in jest.

"If somebody that big, that powerful, and that conniving wants us out, we'd better prepare for a rough ride," I predicted.

'Fuck 'em, if they can't take a joke," Wood quipped.

Somehow, they didn't strike me as having much of a sense of humor.

Over the next two weeks, three devastating but seemingly unrelated events would occur that shocked, disheartened, and scared the hell out of me.

Several days after returning from Chicago, Wood, Ron Mercer, who had flown in from Hawaii, and I sat in my apartment considering our options, or more accurately, our lack of options. It was late evening and we had come from the Starship for this powwow. The knock on the door signaled the start of a three-year battle with the most feared enemy in the country—the IRS.

The two suits properly identified themselves as FBI agents and asked, "Are you Robert Radez?"

"Yes," I answered. Then came the words no one wants to hear:

"You have the right to remain silent. Anything you say can and will be used against you in a court of law. You are entitled to an attorney. If you cannot afford one, one will be provided for. Do you understand your rights?"

My first thought was, "Man, those Bally guys have some serious connections."

Then I thought to ask "Which of my many crimes has brought you here?"

"Failure to file federal income tax returns for the years 1978 and 1979."

"Already?" I yelped incredulously. "Hell, I thought I'd have a couple years to take care of that."

"Normally you would, but someone reported you and that starts the process," he explained. "You have thirty days to respond to these charges." He handed me the legal papers, saying, "Get an attorney—a good one. You're going to need some help."

With that they turned and left. When they read me my rights, I assumed they would take me to some federal dungeon and tell me how the poor were starving and our nation was suffering since I withheld those needed funds. Somehow, the nation had survived, they put me on notice, and the process had begun. I was feeling a little nauseous.

Downright sickness was just around the corner.

That weekend, the Sunday edition of the local Tempe Daily News headlined their second section, "Tempe Today," with the headline "Shattered Fantasy." The accompanying picture showed a table laden with what appeared to be over twenty huge laundry bags laden with, according to the caption, cocaine and marijuana.

The caption read "The two month investigation of Starship fantasy turned up $40, 000 worth of cocaine and marijuana."

The article named the two men who were arrested "…after a two month investigation into reported drug dealing at Starship Fantasy." Later in the article, the reporters quoted the police Sergeant as saying "…after undercover agents gained (the sellers) confidence they set up a second buy of about 3 ½ grams (of cocaine) from (the seller) *at Starship Fantasy. This case was important to us. It was operating out of the Starship* and there's bound to be a lot of contact with juveniles." Similar stories were reported in the Mesa Tribune and The Phoenix Gazette.

Contrary to the report and most important, the drug bust had no connection to the Starship and had actually taken place in the city of Glendale, over 30 miles away on the extreme opposite side of Phoenix. One of the guys arrested was a video mechanic, employed by the company which did maintenance work on our machines. That was the only connection to the Starship, and he didn't even work for us. And it doesn't take a drug dealer to know that a $40,000 bust is small potatoes and not related to the dozens of large laundry or garbage bags shown in the picture.

# Shattered fantasy

## Businessmen jailed in $40,000 drug bust

BY J. PATTERSON O'NEILL
AND BRUCE TRETHEWY
Daily News writers

Two men from Tempe and Phoenix who were arrested after police seized more than $40,000 worth of drugs were released without bond from the city jail Saturday, police said.

Roger Dale Dickman, 26, 1431 E. Baseline Road, and Howard Paul Hughto, 31, of Phoenix were arrested at 5:55 p.m. Friday after officers completed a two-month investigation into reported drug dealing at Starship Fantasy, a Tempe video game arcade at 940 E. Baseline Road.

Dickman was charged with two counts of selling cocaine, one count of possession of cocaine and one count of furnishing marijuana.

Hughto was charged with possession of cocaine for sale, one count of sale of cocaine, one count of possession of marijuana for sale and one count of carrying a concealed weapon.

Police said a preliminary hearing has not been scheduled.

The bust netted more than $40,000 worth of drugs, including 37 pounds of marijuana, an ounce of cocaine, 1,000 valium tablets and 32 vials of hash oil. A 13-member team from Tempe's narcotics squad and Selective Enforcement Unit seized the drugs in three simultaneous busts.

"We hit them just after somebody tipped them off," Sgt. Richard Felice said Saturday. "Dickman was just leaving Hughto's house. We took him a couple of blocks away."

Officers arrested Dickman at the corner of 23rd Avenue and Indian School Road and impounded the van he was driving.

Felice said teams also moved in on Hughto's residence and his business, Ahead Enterprises in Phoenix, within minutes. They seized almost $4,000 in cash from him.

Dickman is vice president of Mercer Manufacturing Supply, 5245 S. Kyrene. The firm is a major supplier of Starship Fantasy's electronic video games.

Last week Mercer was named as a co-defendant — along with the Razwood Corp.,

the firm that owns the Tempe arcade, and Chicago-based KK Industrial Services Corp. — in a civil suit Midway Manufacturing Co. of Illinois filed accusing them of making illegal copies of three Midway video games.

Federal marshals have confiscated 32 machines from the game room to be used as evidence in the suit.

Investigators said they made their first drug buy at the arcade, purchasing about one gram or cocaine after undercover agents gained Dickman's confidence.

They said they set up a second buy of about 3½ grams from Dickman at Starship Fantasy before going to Hughto's home to pick up the cocaine.

Officers bought the drugs then made the arrests.

Felice said three other persons are being sought in connection with the drug sale.

"This case was important to us," Felice said. "It was operating out of Starship, and there's bound to be a lot of contact with juveniles.

"These (cases) are the ones you like to clean up."

We were devastated. Our success was largely due to the squeaky clean reputation we had diligently and purposefully developed. There was no doubt our business would be severely damaged. The newspaper had intentionally constructed the story in a misleading fashion to give a false impression of our involvement. They actually stated that the drug purchase and resulting bust was made at the Starship.

Members of Tempe police narcotics squad and Selective Enforcement Unit log plastic bags containing 37 pounds of marijuana confiscated in a drug raid Friday. The two month investigation of Starship Fantasy turned up $40,000 worth of cocaine and marijuana.

### "The Starship Is Under Attack!"

Monday morning Wood and I were in the editors office demanding a retraction of the story and a clarification that neither we personally nor our business was connected in any way to the drug bust. They agreed, and four weeks later, ran a small "clarification" which referred to the article and stated "Further investigation has revealed police have no record of any drugs actually being purchased on the premises of Starship Fantasy. None of the persons arrested were employed by the Razwood Corp., and there was no intention of implying the ownership was using the arcade as a front for drug sales."

## Starship Fantasy: clarification

On June 28, the Tempe Daily News published a story and photo about the arrests of a Tempe man and a Phoenix man on charges of selling cocaine.

The story referred to an investigation of reported drug dealing at Starship Fantasy, a Tempe video games arcade, and quoted police as saying they made a drug buy at the arcade.

Further investigation has revealed police have no record of any drugs actually being purchased on the premises of Starship Fantasy, which is owned by the Razwood Corp. Actually the arcade was only used as a meeting place by one of the suspects before drugs were to be sold at another location in Phoenix, according to Tempe police documents.

None of the persons arrested were employed by the Razwood Corp., and there was no intention of implying the ownership was using the arcade as a front for drug sales.

"Tempe Daily News Clarification"

When we protested that the clarification was insufficient, they said simply "Sue us."

Within hours we met with our attorneys, one of the Phoenix area's largest and most reputable law firms. We were informed that with the "clarification" by the paper, we lacked sufficient grounds for a lawsuit. Further, their firm had discontinued work on our franchising documentation, believing it could not be accomplished given the negative publicity, and would be unwise for them to continue. Our attorney told us in confidence that the firm had received information from the local federal prosecutor that convinced them we would be shut down.

Their tax attorneys were handling my late filings and IRS matter, adding to the bewildering swirl of events, and we were perplexed by this revelation. Did this problem stem from my tax predicament? Was Midway making good on their thinly veiled threats? Was this a result of the phony news story? Was it possible, just possible, that the drug bust story and the Midway situation were connected? We had no shortage of questions as we left the legal offices. Could anything else go wrong?

Oh yeah.

By Thursday following the drug bust article, our business had gone from full house to the out-house. Only a trickle of customers dared enter our tainted Starship. We decided to begin a public ad campaign, denouncing the misleading article. The paper agreed to take our money for the first full-page ad in the Sunday edition. It was a travesty of justice that we had to pay the very culprits who did us damage, but we designed a fantastic ad. It showed the misleading headline falling apart, and factually disproved the most egregious statements, clearly portraying us as victims of an attempt to stigmatize our business. The response was heartening as the customers began to return within days.

Unfortunately, the days were numbered.

The federal agents arrived in huge semis, with federal court documents authorizing them to seize all electronic games named by Midway Manufacturing as infringing on their patents. They were to be held in storage until a federal court could determine the status of each. When they could get to it, they would have to go through each machine to examine the electronic control boards and make a determination whether they were knock-offs or infringed in any way on U.S. patents. It was estimated to take months.

A flashback of the government putting all Universal Trailer Rental equipment "on hold" was not encouraging.

We were falsely accused of being drug distributors, had a war with the newspaper, watched a multi-million dollar franchise offer go up in smoke, been fired by our attorneys, and our business was an empty building. Oh yeah, and the federal government wanted me for failure to file my taxes. All in all, one hell of a week.

Our discussions centered on finances. Without any revenues from our business, the ongoing rent and other expenses would still continue, making even more difficult the decisions regarding future legal actions. By the time we settled our current legal fees, advertising and wages, virtually all reserves would be expended.

The question being debated was "Do we go into further debt in an attempt to save the seemingly destroyed business." Wood and I felt it was a lost cause. Mercer wanted to hang on, believing the machines would ultimately be returned. After several days of soul searching, Mercer made a good faith proposition to resolve the issue of future direction of the Razwood Corporation.

He offered to buy us out for our original capital investment. Since Wood and I had little hope of the company's survival, we agreed it was a fair offer and accepted. We all parted friends. Eventually, Mercer would sell the Starship to an out-of-state party, recouping his investment.

Wood decided to stay in the Phoenix area and explore the local possibilities. I opted to return to the familiar and comfortable feel of Las Vegas. It seemed something interesting always turned up when I returned there. After all, I was still alive and Vegas was a wonderful place to live.

* * *

# CHAPTER ELEVEN
## ~ Party Times & Little Rhymes ~

I had only been in town for a couple of weeks, once again in a condo on the Las Vegas Country Club, when I met the White Owl girl. Well, not THE White Owl girl of the cigar commercials of that day, but a casino exec with the identical white hair and great looks of the original. A good friend had introduced us one night at Battista's restaurant, a popular spot with the locals as well as entertainers of that era.

Her nickname was Heddy, as in Heddy Lamar, the 1940's and '50's Hollywood sex siren. Or so I thought. She had invited me to stop by the Sand's Hotel/Casino for a drink when she was on duty. Doing so was to lead to two new life experiences, both one-time flings.

She was an exceptionally fit late thirties, a beautiful woman who exuded sexuality. She had the ability to make you pant for her. And I was panting when she invited me in after our first dinner date. Within the first two sips of a drink, we were stripped in her bed, each marveling at the others incredible body. And then I discovered the game behind the name.

She disdained intercourse, preferring and deriving great pleasure from giving head. "Headie," not Heddy, was her self-ordained nickname, a personal inside joke each time she was introduced. She was incredible at it, obviously loving it. It's all she would engage in, but I certainly never felt shortchanged.

And she would get off by bringing me to a climax. If there were a sexual hall of fame, she would surely be inducted under "specialty categories."

The day before New Years, I had been asked to join her and another couple for lunch. Joe and Jodie were friends of hers from Los Angeles. In his 40's, Joe was a physician and Jodie, his slightly younger on-again off-again lover, was a statuesque six-foot tall former dancer from Las Vegas who had found a lucrative career as a fashion model in California. They were very gregarious and the luncheon atmosphere was laid back and filled with enjoyable conversation and a few introductory drinks. We were all warming to the social possibilities of this new friendship and left the restaurant for Headie's apartment to relax and explore the party opportunities for that night, New Year's Eve.

Within 30 minutes and another drink, Joe made a meaningless remark that Jodie interpreted as sexist and demeaning. Her retort triggered a classic example of conflict escalation, each remark becoming more bitter and acerbic until out of control. His final shot was not exactly conciliatory: "Just shut your fucking mouth or I'm going home." She predictably fired back with "Be my guest! I'd rather take a Mexican school bus back to L.A. than make the trip with you."

Without another word, he rose and walked out. The door had barely slammed shut when Jodie said, "Now maybe we can enjoy ourselves." As would be expected, I was somewhat uncomfortable, and mentioned leaving. Both were adamant I stay, virtually pleading that we enjoy the night's celebration together. The conversation once again turned to the evening's planning.

We whiled away the afternoon with idle chatter of possible shows for the evening and a few drinks, then Headie broke out the grass.

I had smoked marijuana on a number of occasions, especially in Hawaii where it was common to see people smoking a joint while walking the street. Nearly every social gathering there provided ample opportunity to sample Maui Wowie or Kona Gold, and I really did enjoy it. The mellow sensation and increased pleasure of the senses was greatly preferable to the aggressive and obnoxious state of booze intoxication. No falling out such as witnessed that day has ever taken place while high on grass. It simply makes everything seem OK, and most things wonderful. But the reality is, its illegal. And the law is so harshly and irrationally stacked against its use that it's not worth the risk. So I was a rare participant, and only in private circles. Kind of like 7 or 8 miles per hour over the speed limit when you know you won't be ticketed for the infraction. Its illegal, but nobody gives a damn.

So we smoked some dope, listened to good music, told absurd tales and laughed the hours away. Despite my occasional mini-step across the legal boundaries, my friends considered me a very "straight" person, and, as such, I had little experience with drugs outside of grass. So when Headie offered me a Quaalude, I was both interested and reluctant, not wanting to ruin my somewhat euphoric state. Both ladies assured me that far from diminishing my high, it would be greatly enhanced by the Quaalude. They each took one, and little persuasion was required for me to join in. It was a first. Later, looking back, I suppose it was part of the plan.

By late evening it was obvious none of us were going anywhere. And I discovered why the drug manufacturers discontinued Quaaludes sometime later. If they affected everyone like they affected me, within a few years every addictive personality on earth—Vegas seemed full of them—would be living in a Quaalude stupor.

I felt so wonderful, so at peace, so totally without concern, that had I been led to the death chamber, I wouldn't have argued. Want my money? Here, take it. Need a car? Use mine. Going to jail? Sounds like fun. Like my shoes? Here, take 'em. "Bob, what would you think of going to bed with Jodie and I?" Sure, sounds good.

WOAH! WHAT? Was that in my head? Was that a real voice? Am I hallucinating?

"I'm sorry Headie, did you just say something?" I heard my voice as I watched the words float across the room to Headie. Good thing, I thought, that I was aimed at her.

"Jodie and I would like to take you to bed and start the New Year out right."

I could see the words like the running news tickers on Times Square. I watched in awe as they entered my head. Then they registered. "Wow." came out. "Wow." There it was again. Only it was more like "Wwooooww." And it was definitely in color. Blues and yellows and greens. Billowy blues, mellow yellow and gorgeous greens.

She had floated toward me and taken my hand. Jodie was gently stroking my other hand and willing me toward the bedroom. Moments later I was convinced I had died. This was otherworldly. It struck me this surely was an out-of-body experience. I looked around but couldn't spot my body elsewhere. The doorway we approached—the bedroom—had no gate and wasn't pearly. Then it occurred to me that maybe this was purgatory. No wonder we can't imagine what heaven is like. My imagination couldn't compute beyond this. If this be purgatory, let me stay awhile and take my punishment like a man.

Stay we did. The combination of drugs and booze made me a very relaxed and uninhibited superman. At first, I was concerned that after an hour or more of incredible love making with two beautiful women, I had not climaxed. Then sanity overcame me and I counted my blessings. So did the women. They counted theirs all night long, moan after moan, shriek after shriek, orgasm after orgasm.

I am quite certain that every man, despite what he may say to the contrary—although I've never heard any man say the contrary—fantasizes about two women. I had a chance to live the fantasy, and under circumstances that I couldn't have even dreamed.

Fate leads some to board an airplane doomed to crash, some to be on the beach for the arrival of a tsunami, others to buy a winning lottery ticket. Fate had dealt me my share of bad hands. Maybe this was a little payback.

I was awakened at 10 AM by the sound of the front door closing. I was in no condition to jump out of bed for any reason, but Headie calmed me with "Its OK. Its just my Mom."

I was laying in the middle of the king size bed with a woman on each side of me, both hands still cradling the stuff of dreams, when Mom walked through the bedroom door. She stood silent for a moment surveying the scene, then said, "Looks like I missed the party," and departed.

Shortly thereafter, fully dressed, I stood in the bedroom doorway on my way out, and with one last look at the gals, ended the fling as it had begun—"Wooooow."

\* \* \*

Since returning to Vegas, I had been asking the "in" crowd for the best tax guy in town. The name of Jack Dalton, CPA came up repeatedly. He was a former IRS agent who specialized in resolving problems for people in predicaments such as mine. I was greatly comforted after giving him the full story on my situation.

I had already filed the late returns. He informed me that the normal procedure was to have the matter transferred to the area of residence in such cases. Mine still being handled out of Hawaii, he would have it transferred to Las Vegas. Once in the Las Vegas office, he could handle it with the IRS and the federal prosecutor. I could expect to plead guilty to the misdemeanors in return for a sentence of probation, and we could then work out some arrangement to pay the $40,000 plus penalties and interest. This was a great relief as the matter was always weighing on my mind. Except for New Year's Eve.

Looking for my next gig, Ron Eckhoff, my good friend who had recommended me for the Hawaii project, suggested I look into buying cars at the Phoenix auto auction for resale to the local car dealers. He had made a living doing it during an interim period earlier, and filled in the blanks for me. The key was getting to know the used car managers at several major new car dealers, and finding out what they would buy. I was surprised to learn that they were interested in specific models and would buy them—at the right price—if I could find them.

I enjoyed this find/buy/sell game for a few months, driving down to Phoenix where I registered as a buyer at the weekly auction, and finding just the right car or cars at the right price, knowing I already had buyers for them. John Duncan was also back in Vegas working for one of the time share houses, and would often make the trip with me, enabling me to buy three vehicles, towing one back behind my car, and John towing a third one behind a second acquisition. At home, I would clean them up, and usually sell them within a few days to my pre-determined used car managers at $300 to $500 profit per vehicle.

I was averaging $600 or $700 per week, working three days. It was a great temporary gig, paying the bills while affording me the time to continue sniffing around for something with appeal. I played golf, rode the dirt bike, and enjoyed late night parties with Headie and friends. And her position with a major hotel/casino provided Headie and I with some exclusive party opportunities. That spring I would enjoy the company of such luminaries as Wayne Newton, Rodney Dangerfield, Rich Little, Johnny Mathis, and many other celebrities of the day.

Headie had become familiar with some of the poems I had written in other times, and often praised them to my embarrassment at these parties, until others, always females, demanded to hear one or more of my ditties. Since most of my poetic efforts were of a personal nature, I penned one specifically generic for such occasions. I titled it:

"A Lesson Learned."

She softly moaned her ecstasy, and made her pleasure clear.
I held her trembling body, then she whispered in my ear.
Did she speak of love? Of soaring the heights?
Did she long for one more time?
Did she pledge undying love for me?
No—she asked me for a rhyme.

I've been around the world and back. Dined with criminals and kings.
My life's been a great adventure, touched by many and wondrous things.
Did she ask of the Queen? Inquire of the Pope?
Did she wonder if I know 'em?
Did she want to know what Carson's like?
No—she asked me for a poem.

Years later now I think of her, her whisper in my ear,
And marvel at the lesson learned from one so sweet and dear.
Need I be rich, or bathed in fame?
Should I be better or worse?
No—to win the heart of a lady fair, I need only come up with a verse.

Now don't get me wrong—I love the ladies. But many of the things they deem important or touching don't even appear on a guy's scale. Which is exactly why guys with questionable motives so easily manipulate some women. Just give 'em what they want emotionally and they are putty to be molded. This bit of poetic fluff, hardly emotional or touching, had an unbelievable effect on some of the party gals.

One, after I recited this ditty to general laughter and polite applause at a party, slinked across the room, stood inches in front of me, grabbed and gently massaged my crotch while saying in a heavy whisper, "I'd love to suck on that while you recite poetry to me."

I somehow managed to respond, "With you sucking on that, I wouldn't even remember my name, let alone any poetry."

Headie rescued me, but I wondered—had I discovered a secret sex weapon? Or just a horny babe?

\* \* \*

I knew Larry Bortels from Hawaii, his headquarters for a significant land syndication operation. While working there a few years prior, I provided some much needed and greatly appreciated professional advice on his planned project to conduct a time-share auction in Seattle, Washington, a hotbed of timeshare activity. He hoped to tap into the growing numbers of owners attempting to sell their time-shares with no feasible outlet to do so. If successful, the auction concept also could have provided another important benefit to our many buyer/owners at the time-share resorts I was running in Hawaii at the time.

The auction was only mildly successful, but established a mutual admiration relationship between Larry and I. Back in Las Vegas, marking time with the auto/wholesaling bit, I was delighted to receive the call from Larry, who, in a business dispute with the State of Hawaii, had moved his entire syndication operation to Golden, Colorado, a Denver suburb. The move was no minor matter since his wife, Leilani, was from Oahu. He urged me to fly up to Colorado for a few days to discuss a potential involvement in one of his syndication projects. The timing was perfect and I'm a sucker for a free trip. I agreed to meet him several days later, in mid-April.

We drove some four hours north out of Denver, into the Rockies of Southern Wyoming, the last hour or more on weather-rutted dirt roads in the middle of nothingness. It provided ample time for Larry to fill me in on his twenty-eight-hundred acre project of wilderness property, tucked into and bordered on three sides by the Medicine Bow National Forrest. He had acquired the property years before through syndication, and was preparing to market it. The property had already been surveyed and subdivided into parcels of ten acres or more. His plan was to maintain the area as wilderness and sell the parcels for camping and hunting.

The property was rugged, forested mountain terrain, ranging from five thousand to sixty-five hundred feet above sea level, only a few miles removed from the rolling, endless expanse leading into the foothills of the majestic Rockies. Entrance to the property was from a county road, dirt, as were all others within forty-five miles. Despite the awesome ruggedness of the surrounding mountainous terrain, the first contact with the property was through a thirty-acre meadow, bordered by the road that loosely followed the far side of a mountain stream that flowed through the meadow. The active beaver dam on the stream had created a "beaver pond" of two or three acres in size, and the meadow and its surrounds presented a scene of breathtaking beauty. Snow was still part of the natural display, and the higher the elevation, the deeper the accumulation. The four log cabins in the meadow were an integral part of the history of this spot, officially appearing on the map as "Squaw Ranch."

In the late 1890's, a pioneer heading west spent some time on an Indian reservation in Oklahoma and became fond of the Chief's daughter. Eventually he asked the Chief for permission to take his daughter west and he was told he must take both she and her sister. He agreed.

Trekking across this mountainous area of Wyoming, he dumped the sister, for whatever reason, on this very spot. The "Squaw," as she became known in the area, made it her home, building a substantial log cabin in the meadow next to the stream, full of trout.

Over time she built a barn, a corral, an irrigation system that channeled water from mountain springs to her elaborate garden, and lived off the land. It is said she accepted help for the heavy lifting from the occasional cowboy or wrangler passing through the area, in return for sharing her many bounties. Thus the area was initially established.

Sometime around 1930, as the Squaw's advancing age made the severe winters more difficult, she traded the property to a Wyoming physician for a house in Casper, Wyoming. Later, during the federal workers program of the 30's known as the WPA, the site was chosen as a camp or work headquarters for crews building the County roads. At that time three more log cabins were built on the property along with an outhouse.

Nearly a half century later, Larry Bortels would purchase the property for a syndication of investors.

Preparing to execute his plan for marketing the property, Larry had the cabins sand blasted to a new-looking condition, installed new flooring and roofing and equipped them with sturdy built-in bunks and Ben Franklin wood burning stoves. No power, no gas, no water, no nonsense.

His idea was to make this meadow area a central headquarters for the convenience of the prospective buyers as well as the owners later on, turning one of the cabins into a "bathhouse" with running water from a well, facilitating showers and commodes.

Larry presented me with a two-pronged proposition. First, he wanted me to help develop a marketing plan to draw prospective campers and hunters out of the Denver area. Then he hoped that I would stay on the property for the summer, showing and selling the parcels that were spread throughout the twenty-eight-hundred acres of the dense wilderness to those enticed there by the marketing program.

Of course, the primitive conditions made the proposition seem absurd. At first. Even with a generous piece of the deal, it was inconceivable. But I had to admit, as Larry pushed his 4-wheel-drive Blazer to the limits, scaling mountain walls, fording streams, squeezing through the forest and coaxing it through the snow—this was the most serene, majestic and incredible spot I had ever seen up close and personal.

Late that afternoon, winding down into the more typical barren, rolling Wyoming terrain thirty minutes from the property, we stopped to watch herd after herd of antelope, sixty, eighty, one hundred of them in a herd, peacefully grazing several hundred yards off the road. And before we were back in Denver, I knew that I had visited a very special place.

Back in Las Vegas, armed with all the pertinent information, I had to make the decision. Was I insane to even consider it? Despite my appreciation for comfort, I do love the out of doors, abundant with nature's many pleasures and surprises. And like most, I am truly captivated by wildlife. Maybe it wasn't so farfetched.

My youngest son, Michael, would be entering his senior year at SMU that fall, and his first three years there had offered scarce opportunity for much time together. I saw this as a potential opportunity to share a great and unique adventure. He had always thrilled over my motorcycle exploits, and had jumped at the rare chance for some limited riding on several occasions when visiting me in the past. With three months in the wilderness, riding every day chasing after his dad, he could hone his riding skills while having a fantastic summer.

I invited him to join me, help in the overall task that awaited, and share a once in a lifetime opportunity with me. He excitedly agreed. The decision was made.

By June 1st, I had found and bought the perfect Yamaha 250 YZ for Mike. The 250 YZ was an exceptional motorcycle made specifically for riding off-road, in the dirt. It was powered by a 250 cc engine that is powerful in its own right, but easily souped up. It was equipped with a special racing exhaust pipe and would run with my 460 YZ—a similar but slightly larger and more powerful machine—while being easier to handle. My motorcycle trailer had a large tool chest attached, ample for the tools and some spare parts we might need. I leased a 4-wheel drive Ford Bronco, necessary to get to and access the Wyoming property. We loaded all our personal and survival gear in the Bronco, hooked up the loaded trailer and left for the summer.

It was one of life's great experiences. It could never happen again, and we knew it. We savored it. Every day was an adventure of unexpected surprises. Using the bikes, we were able to find and identify all the parcels and to learn the scratched out paths, which provided access to them. Each day we would marvel at the profound numbers and varieties of animals; numerous deer, eagles, game both small and large, furred and feathered.

We improved our quality of life greatly with the addition of a propane refrigerator and tank. This enabled us to keep perishables that we secured from weekly trips to Douglas, Wyoming, about forty-five miles and over ninety minutes to the north. It took a four-wheeler to navigate the dirt road, continually washed out by the near daily noontime thunderstorms.

We also ran small plastic tubing through our cabin to the propane tank, providing a lantern light source in the evening. The nights without lights reintroduced me to the sheer blackness of total dark I had not seen since Korea.

We established responsibilities. Each morning I would brave the frosty chill to build a fire in the potbelly stove, and Mike did the cooking. The standard response to the desired breakfast was "trout and eggs." This wasn't so much a real desire for trout as a constant reminder that Mike was committed to catching a trout from the stream that traversed the property.

The water was crystal clear and you could see the trout. However, they could also see you. He tried every day. After a couple weeks, I picked up a fly rod during one of our forays into Douglas, and that night told Mike if he would start the fire in the morning, we would indeed have trout and eggs for breakfast.

The following morning I woke Mike as I left the cabin at the crack of dawn, telling him to start the fire. He was more than incredulous. In the preceding days I had already done my due diligence on the pond, making a mental note of the best spots for success with the fly rod. It was only some fifty yards to one of the previously determined spots on the beaver pond. I had the fly rod, one fly, a pail and a knife.

The fly had barely landed on the very first cast before it was engulfed in a swirl of water, the rod bending to the sudden pressure of the determined trout. Two casts produced two 14-inch brook trout. I cleaned them on the spot, returning to the cabin within minutes of having left. Mike was still in his bunk but came wide-awake when I tantalized him with the fish. That day, he learned to fly fish.

We hired a water witcher to find a well site, and began constructing some basic dividers in the "bath house" cabin. We built a man's and a woman's shower and sink area, and after weeks of bathing in the icy waters of a nearby waterfall, prayed to find a producing well. When the well digger hit water, we had it piped to the bath house, attached a gas generator to a water pump, hooked up the supply to the plumbing in the bath house which included a propane water heater with a pressure bladder. The pump would fill the heater tank, expanding the bladder as it filled which created the water pressure for the showers and sinks. Each day we would run the generator for an hour or so to fill the heater tank, light the propane and voila—HOT WATER.

Hot showers never felt so good. We had been bathing in the frigid waterfall, albeit on a less regular basis than usual, for fifty days.

We took pictures of the elk herd we saw routinely on a neighboring property, and determined it had about one hundred fifty head. Our "neighbor" was a Wyoming legend, John Bell. He had started his ranch as a nineteen-year old with a few acres of land and a few head of steer. Fifty-six years later at age seventy-five, his ranch measured nearly seven miles by nine miles and contained five thousand head of steer. It included some of the rolling flatlands where we would zoom the bikes into a herd of antelope, cull out a big stag and run alongside him for several minutes, watching him watching us, thundering over the countryside at sixty-five miles per hour, us marveling at his incredible strength and grace in flight, he no doubt in shocked amazement that something could keep up with him. It was something to behold. After a minute or two of such chase, we would abandon the pursuit, and excitedly exchange takes on the adrenalin pumping experience before returning to the herd for another.

"Mike with Rescued, Hours-Old Antelope"

We rode daily, following the small trails carved through the forest by the deer, dropping to the valley floor, across a mountain stream to a meadow strewn with spring wild flowers, never knowing where the trail would take us. When we chanced upon a long abandoned trapper's shack, we would stop to explore it, imagining who had occupied it and how he lived, how he traveled to this spot. Then back up through the stands of birch trees, out to the edge of a cliff, with a spectacular view of incredible scenery that never ended. Certainly, this was God's back yard, and we were blessed to play in it.

"Gettin' It On!"

On our way again, dicing wildly down an old jeep trail or seldom seen fire break, dodging the occasional startled deer, both vying for the lead to be the first through the numerous mud puddles that would douse the follower, urging us faster and faster. By the end of summer, Mike was a fairly accomplished rider. It was an idyllic time like no other, in an idyllic place like no other, with a bonding quality like no other.

The marketing scheme for the property never clicked, and business-wise, it was a dud. But from a life standpoint, I spent 90 days with my son who was about to go off into a life of his own. We shared a phenomenal experience that will bind us for life. It was invaluable beyond imagination. Then it was over.

"Bob & Mike—Mountain Men"

\* \* \*

Heading back home to Las Vegas, I deluded myself into thinking it was back to the real world. Upon arrival, I became quickly aware that it was back to the fringe of the real world. Jack Dalton, my IRS expert, informed me that the Honolulu IRS refused to transfer my case out of Hawaii, and I would be prosecuted in a Honolulu court. He claimed this was a first in his twenty-year experience, indicating something very unusual was underway. He strongly urged me to retain a Honolulu attorney, and preferably one of Japanese heritage, since the legal system there, like Oahu society in general, is dominated by the Japanese/American population. Taking his advice, I flew to Honolulu for a sit-down with my good friend and former partner, Rick Steere, who had an inside line on all things local.

It was great to be back in Hawaii, catching up with my buddy Rick, but I was stunned when he revealed the source of my IRS problem. Our former boss, Rodney Inaba, had, without my knowledge, somehow determined that I had attempted to undermine him with his Canadian business partners/investors. Outraged, he sought revenge. He had asked friends of his with the

IRS to check my tax records, and had conspired with other friends in the prosecutor's office as well as the IRS to avenge the imagined betrayal of him. The "good ol' boy" system was alive and well in Hawaii. I was, after all, a Las Vegas Howlie.

I retained the Japanese/American attorney recommended by Rick, and left the matter in his hands. The primary goal was to get the matter transferred to Las Vegas.

I would spend the remainder of the year in Reno Nevada, helping a friend construct a time-share program for a downtown hotel that his group was acquiring. In the end, their acquisition failed and I was back in Las Vegas for the New Year, 1983. It had been another roller coaster year.

\* \* \*

"Bob, this is Frank Braglia. You're a hard man to track down."

Frank was one of the few old-school guys from the land business that I respected. He had been part of the upper echelon in management when I got involved 14 years prior, and became a kingpin in the marketing end of the industry, controlling the many booking locations throughout Las Vegas. Some 10 years my elder, I admired his calm, soft-spoken approach. I pictured him as a "Don," the Godfather of Las Vegas marketing. I hadn't spoken to him in years.

"How nice to hear from you, Frank. Yeah, it's been a busy year. Just got back from a little stint in Reno. Where are you now, and to what do I owe this honor?"

"I'm in Atlantic City, and I'm on top of an off-site operation on the boardwalk for Wayne Newton."

"Wayne Newton the Singer?" I asked incredulously. "Last I heard he was trying to buy the Aladdin Hotel here in Vegas."

"Yeah, the singer," he confirmed. "He's committed $25 million to a time share project in the Poconos, and we're selling his program here. Bob, we'd like to fly you out here to take a look at our operation and discuss the possibilities."

"What possibilities are you talking about, Frank?"

"Well, we have a few problems on the sales side of this deal. I have the best locations tied up for booking units (prospective customers), but honestly, our sales force is a joke. We need some help, and I know you're the best."

"Frank," I said with all the sympathy I could muster, "I just came back from Reno, which is the armpit of America. About the only place worse I know of is Atlantic City, the asshole of the earth. I can't imagine anything that would convince me to do a deal there. Let me try to find someone hungry for a deal right now that might consider a gig in a shit hole."

"Hey Bob," he countered, "What do you have going so hot that you can't even listen to a proposition?"

"OK, you've got me there," I admitted, "but the Northeast is not my kinda place."

"Bob, grab a plane, come out for a couple days. We'll pick up the tab for everything. I know the best restaurants in town, you'll be a VIP, spend a little time with Wayne Newton, talk a little business, see what we've got going, then decide whether to consider a deal. What do you have to lose?"

\* \* \*

The limo waiting for me at the Philadelphia airport for the drive to Atlantic City was a good start. Seeing Frank again was also a plus. And dinner with Braglia is always an Italian extravaganza. The VIP treatment at the Wayne Newton show that night was admittedly impressive, as was meeting with him later in such a personal setting. I'd had an earlier opportunity to meet Newton at a private party in Las Vegas, and then, as now, he was warm and friendly beyond expectations. Hey, the guy was the top entertainer in Las Vegas at the time, and that meant top in the world. Damn right I was impressed. Frank was waging one hell of a campaign.

The sales facility was quite nice, a second floor layout in a hotel property right on the boardwalk.

I was familiar with the sales manager through industry scuttlebutt, but had never met him. From what I'd heard, I assumed Frank couldn't find anyone else to go there. The guy's wife was the assistant manager. It was a mess; the worst I'd seen. The operation had lost nearly $600,000 in its first three months. Could I recover it? Could I make it work? Would I? Pretty please?

The offer was reasonable. Certainly not a home run, but reasonable. In the end, it wasn't the offer that got me. It wasn't the VIP treatment or even the genuine good-guy assurances of Wayne Newton. What intrigued me was knowing that I would have to completely rebuild the sales force from the management on down. The task seemed overwhelming. That was exciting,

In truth, having nothing going at the time certainly played a role in the decision. The general plan that was formulating in my head over the next few days, if successfully executed, could have me out of there in as little as 90 days. That was tolerable. I packed my bags.

The first ten days in the operation was spent observing, asking questions and, especially, listening to the answers. I quickly determined that management had set up a system that scammed the company. They would essentially say whatever necessary to write business, but 80% of it cancelled during the state mandated rescission period. They would not forward or report the rescissions to the home office, enabling the cancelled deals to process and commissions to be paid. Months would pass before detection. By the time I arrived, the proverbial manure was making daily contact with the corporate fan. The whole operation stunk. I fired the managers unceremoniously.

The best chance for success was to virtually start over. Unlike other established resort areas, Atlantic City had no time-share talent pool. Top producers could work where they chose, and no super-stars chose Atlantic City. My track record of success had earned a sterling reputation in the industry, especially with those who had worked with me in the past. The pros knew they would not only make money in my projects, but always receive their money without hassle and be treated fairly and with respect. That reputation would be vital in convincing the people I wanted to seriously consider Atlantic City.

My first call was to Rick Wood. Since the Starship Fantasy was grounded, we had talked on occasion. He was still in the Phoenix area and was involved with a local time share effort that was hanging on by a thread. I gave him the full picture of my new project, then shared my vision of a "reunion."

"Rick, think of the fun we had building a dynamic machine in Hawaii. The people who worked on your team loved every minute of it, and I'm convinced some of them would welcome the opportunity for another run. With both of us involved, we can assemble a super sales force, make this into a killer deal, and have a ball doing it. Not only that, but once its up and running and I've honored my commitment to the Newton people, I'll turn the whole deal over to you."

"Bob, you know it'll take awhile to get commissions flowing. It would be asking a lot for those people to trade Hawaii for Atlantic City. But their expense of getting there and then staying alive till commissions are payable makes it unrealistic."

"I've got it all covered. I was able to convince the principles here that this "construction phase" would have to be funded. I'll pay to fly our people in, put them up in hotels for 30 days and front some walk-around money. They will have to get a New Jersey real estate license, but I've arranged for a crash course and fairly quick testing, all paid for. Meantime, they can still sell, but not close. You and I as company employees will handle the act of money changing hands. Its all legal, approved and worked out. Whaddaya say?"

It took a couple days, but Rick came aboard with typical enthusiasm. I told him to start the ball rolling by calling Eileen Cashmere, the Super-Pro from our Hawaiian crew. Once she agreed, the word got out and the calls started coming with others wanting in. Bringing people that distance and subsidizing them for a month was a costly proposition, so we had to be very selective whom we would invite or accept. The contrasting benefit, however, was that two weeks later, we had assembled a formidable crew of very motivated top professionals.

After several days of product and systems training, we were in business. As a seasoned master motivator by then, I had them primed for success from the opening bell. As a show of confidence, I had spelled out on a chalkboard the progressively optimistic production goals for the coming three months, complete with the total commissions, bonuses and perks that would be up for grabs as a result. All these projections were considered insanity by the few hold-overs of the previous regime. They were about to be introduced to excellence.

In the following 90 days, all outlined goals would be met or exceeded.

About the time everyone was assembled and training had begun, I received a call from A. P. Howe, in Hawaii and broken hearted. So he said. All the top hitters he had worked with for years had been invited to an exciting "reunion project" in New Jersey, for his "good friend" Bob Radez, and he was left behind.

"Baub," he said dejectedly in that haughty British accent, "how could you overlook me. You know very well that I'm the best closer in Hawaii. I can't tell you how disappointed I am."

"AP, how many times did I fire you?"

"Three times," he said.

"And how many times did one of the other managers fire you?"

"Baub, you know my memory's not that good when I'm drunk."

"AP, New Jersey is a long way from Hawaii. Its costing me an arm and a leg to bring people all the way out here and put them up for a month, and you know you couldn't last a month. I'd never recoup the expense of bringing you out. Your drinking problem is deep seated and unarguable."

"Baub," he said calmly, "I will acknowledge that in the past I've had a problem with booze, but I swear to you, I've solved the problem."

"AP, are you gonna look me in the phone and tell me that you're no longer drinking, and worse yet, expect me to believe it?"

"No, not at all" he said. "I said I've solved *my* problem with booze—I've found a liquor store that's open 24 hours a day, so I no longer have a problem."

When I finally quit laughing, I had to admit to myself that I loved AP Howe. He was simply one of the most charismatic and loveable drunks in the world. And he held the world record for the worst "choke" in the history of golf. Once, playing in a foursome with Wood, Faraone and myself, he had a putt of 8 inches on the last hole for all the money, and yipped it so bad it traveled only four inches. He never lived it down, but thereafter, every mention of it was followed by hysterical laughter. He was too much fun. I arranged for him to join us.

AP sold a deal every day. He was inspirational to the team. For two weeks. Our first sales party of the day was at 10 AM, and we started each day with a mandatory sales meeting at 9 AM to discuss the previous day's business, what we might learn from it, hand out spiffs and generally get fired up for the day ahead. The only acceptable excuse for being late to my sales meeting was proof of death the night before.

One fateful day, AP showed up just as I was finishing up the meeting about 9:45. He was very visibly bombed and disheveled, his already reddened face even puffier than usual, his eyes so red he could have stopped traffic just by blinking them. His aloha shirt displayed the many colors of his favorite foods from the previous twelve hours, and the pattern of cigarette burns rendered it a see-through quality. His lap must have served as an ashtray during the night's activities, considering the numerous holes providing ventilation for his underwear. Upon entering, he stood momentarily in front of the assemblage, swaying noticeably, glanced at his wrist where presumably a watch had once rested, and finally announced, "I must have overslept." The entire room erupted in laughter. It was the second day in a row. It was also his last.

I wouldn't see AP Howe again for seven years.

The administration staff had been retained in its entirety. It consisted of five women who handled all the typing, contracts, records, in-house accounting and secretarial work, as well as serving as "Hostesses," providing our guests coffee, soft drinks and general hospitality. All were fairly young and attractive, but I strictly adhere to a no- involvement policy with employees, so would never entertain an intimate relationship. However it is also my policy to develop a close and cordial working relationship with every member of my organization.

One of the staff, a very ebullient young blond named Robin did attract my attention. Intentionally. She doted on me, bringing coffee, never a requisite of my staff, and attending to every perceived desire. Although my taste in women is diverse, my preference runs toward the smallish, petite type. Even if I were to consider an interest beyond professional, she did not fit my "preference profile," although her voluptuous, "Marilyn Monroe" similarity was unmistakable and hard to ignore. At twenty, she was approximately my daughter's age. Nevertheless, I was captivated by her upbeat attitude. And a little "eye candy" is nice to have around.

When I initially drove into town to undertake this project, I had found and leased a nice condo on the beach in Margate, a fairly upscale area on the outskirts of A.C. I had no idea at the time that it was considered a prestige address. For me, it was a place to sleep, hang clothes and park my car. To Robin, an impressionable young lady struggling with the economic realities of adulthood and sharing a small apartment with four other young women, my address represented wealth and status.

Having recently spent a few years in Hawaii, and being a confirmed "West Coast" kind of guy, I was greatly put off by the local beach scene. The sand wasn't appealing, and the muddy looking ocean waves deposited unseemly refuse, including dead sea animals, on the beach. In a word, I found it disgusting. That's why I was surprised when Robin asked one day if I minded that she use the beach behind my building.

My first thought and response was, "For what?"

She looked at me quizzically and answered "Just to walk in the sand and maybe lay in the sun. You know, beach time."

"Beach time? On that beach?" I queried. "Robin, there's trash washing up on the shore, a bunch of ugly dead sea animals of some kind, with round shells and long tails strewing the beach, and I just heard on the news that bags of hypodermic needles, probably disposed of by a hospital, were found washed up on the beach. You want to walk on that beach?"

"Bob," she said patiently, " those dead animals are horseshoe crabs that show up this time of year. And the needles made the news because something like that is a rarity. In another month or so, millions of people will flock here for the beach. What's the matter with you?"

"They don't go in that water, do they?" I asked.

"Of course they do. This is Atlantic City. This is the beach and the boardwalk and the ocean that they come for."

"Kid," I said, "you've got to get out of here and see the West Coast. You need to see what a beach looks like, and an ocean so clear and blue that it invites you in rather than dares you to risk it."

"Well, if I ever have the chance, I'll jump at it." She was quite emphatic.

I remembered how anxious I was to go West years earlier, and actually felt sorry for her, probably trapped in this (to me) less than desirable environment during these important years of her life. I also knew that when my work in A.C. was done, I would most likely head to California to meet an old friend with a new project. John Faraone, whom I had convinced to run my new sales room in Hawaii five years earlier, had called me several times since I started the Wayne Newton deal. He was in Palm Springs, California, running a very upscale time-share operation on a golf course, and was encouraging me to come out for some discussions.

"Robin, I may end up in California in a couple months. If I made it possible for you, would you really want to travel west?"

Her reply was immediate. "Hell Yes!"

\* \* \*

# CHAPTER TWELVE
## ~ Do the Right Thing Because It's Right ~

There are exceptional salespeople. There are exceptional closers. There are exceptional sales managers. Extremely rare is the person who encompasses all three. John Faraone was that rare exception. He was one of the best at each, and the absolute best I'd ever known at combining the necessary skills of all. Which is why I was more than curious at his near-weekly calls, encouraging me to come to Palm Springs California. He told me in many different ways that he was on top of a super deal in the making, but that he simply wasn't "motivated." He steadfastly maintained he could see the tremendous potential and knew I could make it materialize.

Palm Springs is the desert playground of the Southern California wealthy. It could also be considered the golf capital of the West, boasting at that time nearly 100 courses. As much of a golf-nut as I had become, I had never been to Palm Springs. But it was definitely preferable to Atlantic City to me.

The Wayne Newton off-site sales center had gone together nicely with the expected insurmountable problems ultimately being resolved. It never ceased to amaze me how many catastrophes had to be overcome to make one of these operations successful.

In reflection, I was profoundly impressed how much could be accomplished by talented people combining their efforts in pursuit of common goals. And just how important organizational, motivational and management skills were in the leadership of such pursuits. My confidence levels were at an all time high, having turned this monumental loser into a major winner. The office was doing over $1,500,000 in monthly sales by the end of May, which also marked about ninety days since we started sales.

The lost monies of the original operation were virtually guaranteed to be recouped, and this organization was on an established path of profitability. I had kept Rick Wood involved in the critical path of the business so that a smooth transition was a certainty. It was time to say goodbye. I had begun California dreamin'.

\* \* \*

I got bad news; I got good news. Bad: the IRS office in Honolulu absolutely refused to transfer my case out of Hawaii. According to my CPA and my Hawaii attorney, this was unprecedented. I had made Rodney Inaba a wealthy man, and in return, he was pulling strings to nail me for an imagined grievance. Good: the attorney reported that the feds were amenable to a guilty plea in return for a one-year probation.

I would be required to make several court appearances in Honolulu to accomplish this. In the meantime, we were still attempting to negotiate a settlement on the amount owed for those two years, with the IRS claiming outrageous sums far beyond reason. It was a problem of my own making, and I would have to handle it in the best way possible. I had salted away over $30,000 from the Atlantic City venture, and hoped that would resolve my IRS debt. It seemed they were more interested in making unrealistic demands than in collecting what I owed. Meantime, life had to go on.

Palm Springs is truly an oasis in a vast sea of sand. The endless hues of tan merely provide contrast to the emerald green checkerboard of golf courses and lawns, the pattern stitched together by the lines of palm trees and an endless array of swimming pools. The entire mosaic is enhanced by the border of mountains, protecting it all from being blown away by the dry desert winds.

On this June 10th, my first glimpse of this golfing Mecca was accompanied by the pleasant combination of excitement and anticipation. This was my kind of place, a warm, dry climate feeding the constant holiday/relaxation/party atmosphere. Much like Hawaii in that everybody feels good about being here and being alive, and I felt very good and very alive. I liked this place.

I had talked to Faraone earlier that morning, agreeing to meet with him at the resort. Driving onto the resort grounds, I was impressed. While not extravagant or ostentatious, the entrance conveyed a distinct sense of class and comfort. The project had been a hotel on the Palm Springs Golf Course, but after acquisition was converted into sumptuous, dollhouse condominiums.

Although we talked often, I had not seen Faraone since leaving Hawaii. Aside from my professional respect and admiration of Faraone, I considered him to be one of my few close personal friends. This reunion was more than an opportunity for a new venture. It was a get-together of two good friends.

A tour of the resort convinced me it had all the ingredients for a successful time-share project. Faraone filled me in on the details. The original hotel had been purchased by "The Glen Ivy Financial Group," a corporation privately owned by Ralph Mann. Mann had formed his company eight years earlier upon moving from Wisconsin to Southern California. He had been a building contractor and aspired to become a California developer. He began his California business career with the purchase of a debilitated mobile home park several miles south of Riverside, in a spot called Glen Ivy. Upgrading the property, Mann converted it into a motor home park, selling the spaces on a bastardized time-share-like program.

He became enamored of the time-share concept and bought a small 15 unit condo project in Palm Springs for time-sharing. Having no background or real skills in the sales side of business, he was at the mercy of outside sales outfits, and suffered through three years of sales efforts to finally sell out the 15 units. Undeterred by the numerous difficulties, toward the final stages of that project he had acquired the golf course hotel property for conversion to condos. His search for help in the sales arena led him to Faraone, who in turn imported several suede shoe sharks out of Vegas to form a sales team.

Located an easy 90 minutes from L.A. and barely two hours from San Diego, Palm Springs encompasses 16 million people for marketing purposes. For a resort area, that's astronomical. What's more, the prospects responding to the mailed solicitations to attend a sales presentation at the resort were arriving in Mercedes, Cadillacs and other luxury cars. This deal had everything going for it, and yet it was struggling. Uncharacteristically, Faraone had surrendered to failure even while recognizing the rare potential of the project. Over the next few hours, I would find out why.

Even though he was from an upper-middle class family, John Faraone had grown up on the streets of New York, and had a propensity to admire the wild side of life. Palm Springs was a center of the well-to-do wild side. The most prominent nightclub was the "Volcano," a disco of the times, located barely a block from the resort. Each night the Volcano parking lot was full of Lincolns and Cadillacs and such, but the valet parking was filled with Ferraris, Lamborghinis, Rolls Royces and the like, and stretch limos lined their designated area.

Inside the Volcano, the trappings of the wealthy were everywhere. In 1983 that meant cocaine in abundance. John was always enamored of this lifestyle in film. Now he had his fling at living it. He had become part of the "scene." The scene embraced the drug culture. Of course, since it was the drug culture of the wealthy, it was chic.

John had urged me to Palm Springs not only because I was the most capable person he knew, but the most self disciplined. He knew that, in spite of constant exposure, I had never abused or overindulged in booze or drugs, and would not fall victim to the allure that held him captive. Over the next 10 days, I would discover how entrenched the problem was.

The renovated hotel time-share resort was named "The Plaza of Palm Springs." It was referred to in some circles as "The Coke Connection." And for good reason. Ralph Mann had a money partner in the Plaza—his father-in-law, Ron Lawson. Ron had a colorful past. He had been a major player in the phone-room scams that had been busted by the feds in Las Vegas several years earlier. He had operated on a large scale and reportedly came away with over thirty million dollars. He had been arrested, charged and tried, but was acquitted.

He came to Palm Springs, invested in his son-in-law's new hotel/condo conversion, and ended up in charge of marketing. This entailed mail and other programs to attract prospects to the sales presentations. As such, he worked on a daily basis with Faraone who quickly and enthusiastically became his coke-and-carouse buddy. Most of Faraone's small sales force had followed their lead. The Plaza had become a coke-house.

I had a frank sit-down with John, pleading with him to get straightened out. He was in the process of flushing himself down the crapper, while on the verge of serious success. I told him I would take over the sales, build a dynamo, and sell out the project in one year. All he had to do was go away somewhere and get clean, He could retain all the profits to which he was entitled, simply giving me a point or two overwrite. While he didn't say it directly, I could see that he was enjoying his role as a self-perceived player in the Palm Springs "scene," and wasn't ready for rehabilitation.

Meanwhile, it was not unusual to see John, unshaven, resplendent in a tie-dye t-shirt, blue jean cut-offs and a bandana wrap on his head, literally staggering down the main hallway of the Plaza in mid-afternoon with Ron Lawson, both so loaded they were in another world. Ron would unabashedly be toting a large zip- lock bag full of coke, oblivious to guests or member/ owners. I suppose there were deals to be made.

John's attraction to the seedier side of society was underscored by his choice of "Super Fly" as his favorite movie. It painted pimps and drug dealers in glowing colors. Ironically, Ron Lawson was a character befitting a role in such a flick. He was a high roller, said to be leasing 12 Lincoln automobiles for the 12 women he had stashed in 12 different apartments. They were there for the taking. And the coke. With the Plaza being known as the Coke Connection, it was only fitting that Ron was called the "Coke King" of Palm Springs.

When I first arrived, John had slipped me $1000 and asked me to nose around and do what I could to make it happen. I was unsure how I would handle this overall situation, but spent a great deal of time in those first few days becoming familiar with the people, the project and the systems involved. It grieved me to see the obvious potential so abused and squandered. Certainly, I was not going to be part of the status quo.

John Smith was the resort's General Manager, in charge of the owner/ member check-ins, reservations, restaurant, bar, spa and all other hotel type activities. Knowing my fondness for golf, he invited me to be his guest at the Mission Hills Resort course, where the Dinah Shore Invitational, one of the "majors" on the LPGA tour was played. It was the first in a series of meetings that would lead to my becoming a multi-millionaire

We played 18 holes, but it was a secret meeting to feel me out on behalf of Ralph Mann, on my interest in developing a sales organization for him at the Plaza. They had checked me out and knew of my track record in making lemonade from lemons. They also knew Faraone was my friend. Understandably, Smith and Mann strongly urged my confidentiality. I pledged it, and instructed him to set up a meeting with Ralph.

\* \* \*

Ralph Mann was a big teddy bear kind of guy with an easy-going manner about him. He was the owner, President and CEO of the Glen Ivy Company. They weren't exactly setting records in the time-share industry, and its future was in grave doubt. He didn't exude an air of sophistication, but rather a down-to-earth, matter of fact, straight talk quality. Early on in our conversations I developed a comfortable feeling of trust with him. Very rare, possibly unique, was his recognition that the arena of sales was beyond his comprehension, and he was prepared to give me the reins and seriously consider any and all recommendations or suggestions I might make. He would install me as Director of Sales. But he wanted John Faraone gone.

I assured him that if I accepted the position, I would discuss all matters requiring significant expenditures and would approach my position as if I were a partner in the business, but that I would make all decisions regarding systems, personnel and other sales matters. But I wanted Ron Lawson gone.

Furthermore, I could not agree to simply kicking Faraone out of the deal, although it was obvious he could no longer remain over the sales department.

Ralph pointed out that removing Ron would result in a critical cash crunch, he being the sugar daddy. Sales had only reached a monthly high of $250,000 once, and the marketing costs alone, exclusive of sales costs, were eating 50% of gross revenues. Cost of product, actual sales expenses, financing charges, all were completely out of whack.

I had a simple solution. Generate a minimum of a million dollars per month in sales.

I guaranteed Ralph that I would create a cash flow necessary to carry the deal, and he could defer payment of my 2% overwrite that I would want, until the cash flow was there to allow it. I would also work with Ralph personally to increase the efficiency of the marketing programs, which would be run or directly supervised by Ralph since that's the single largest expense in the business.

These were the issues we discussed over the next two meetings. Ralph could sense I had a firm grip on the matters, and he had few doubts that I could deliver. He finally agreed to sever his ties with Ron, and even came up with a plan for Faraone. Ralph would fund a storefront OPC operation on the main street in Palm Springs for Faraone to run. OPC is short for "outside personal contact," as differentiated from mail and telephone solicitation marketing programs. Faraone's storefront would display many items such as small TVs, cameras and dinner tickets, which would be offered free for attending our sales presentation. All concerns of both sides were satisfactorily resolved, and it was apparent that Ralph and I worked well together. Our mutual optimism bode well for the future of the Plaza and Glen Ivy Financial.

I immediately began the groundwork for once again building a sales team. At the same time, Ralph and I laid out our plans to Faraone, who was agreeable to the OPC program. The matter of booting Ron was left to Ralph—a family affair.

Even though Palm Springs had a couple other sizable time-share operations and a fairly adequate talent pool, recruitment of top rung sales people was virtually impossible due to the "coke house" reputation of the Plaza. Importing talent would be required since I planned to retain few of the existing sales people. I didn't want to undercut Rick Wood, but I wanted a few of the people we had beckoned to New Jersey. Rick cooperated as "pay-back" for my setting him up with the Atlantic City deal. Convincing the chosen few to depart Atlantic City for Palm Springs and a project on the golf course with me at the helm was more like offering gifts than asking favors. Between the "imports," the ones I retained, a few I invited from Las Vegas, and a few locals who heard I was taking over, we soon were a force of 18.

In the meantime, I had leased a beautiful townhouse on one of the opulent country club courses in neighboring Ranch Mirage. A spacious two-bedroom ranch-style casa in a gate-guarded community, it was furnished in elegant but comfortable decor. The relaxing ambiance and lush breathtaking surroundings led me to thoughts of Robin, stuck in Atlantic City, and her certain awe at such a lifestyle.

As a teen, like so many her age, she had endured an uncomfortable and often volatile relationship with her mother. At seventeen, a year after her parent's divorce, she welcomed the opportunity to live with her father. At eighteen she entered college, but the following year her father's decision to remarry resulted in serious disagreements, ending with Robin being asked to leave. She dropped out of college, found a job and began the harsh reality of individual responsibility without adequate preparation. I was all too familiar with the scenario and couldn't help but be sympathetic. I placed the call.

"Well, here's your chance" I said after the opening banter, as if honoring my earlier promise. Actually, it was very superficial since it was unlikely this born and bred New Jersey twenty-year old would pack up and move across the country into unknown circumstances.

"If you're serious about getting out of that area, here's what I'll do. I'll fly you out to Palm Springs. I won't hire you because of the distractive talk it would create in my organization. But with your experience you won't have any problem getting a job at one of the other resorts. If that doesn't work out to your satisfaction, and if you want to, I'll send you to Las Vegas with a letter of introduction to every time share project there. You'll be able to pick and choose where you want to work. And if you're just not happy with any of it, I'll fly you back to New Jersey. Meantime, I've got a little two bedroom place here where you are welcome to stay till you get on your feet."

"I told her you'd call," she said.

"Told who?" I asked.

"My Mom. I told her you'd call and that if things worked out for you and you invited me that I was going. She said I was naive, no way you'd even call, let alone actually invite me out."

"Well, she was half right" I said. "You are naive. But I didn't think when it came right down to it, you would leave."

"Boy, were you wrong. I'll give a two weeks notice tomorrow. Arrange my flight anytime after that." She was bubbling over with excitement.

* * *

Robin stepped off the plane looking as if she had barely escaped the clutches of the grim reaper. She had been ill for most of her flight. The feel of terra firma under her feet, the sunshine and clear sky, the surrounding majestic mountains all contributed to her quick recovery.

As we drove across the city through the palm tree-lined streets onto Bob Hope Drive in Rancho Mirage California, she was in awe of the surroundings. The very names of the street, community and state are impressive to a young lady from Vineland New Jersey. But entering the gate guarded golf community, passing by and being mesmerized by the water fountains spraying columns of glistening prisms skyward into the pristine sunshine, descending back to form ripples in the mirror-like scenic ponds amidst the manicured lawns and fairways—that was overwhelming. She was in mouth-opened silence as we pulled into the driveway of her new, if temporary digs. I expected some comment of approval, but she never uttered a word for nearly an hour.

She would tell me later that she had been so incredibly awed with the entirety of the experience, she was literally struck dumb.

Can there be a greater gift?

* * *

During the initial organizational stages with my crew, I conducted a special meeting at which my heartfelt address set the tone for a different style, a different approach, and, in retrospect, a new and different era in the industry. It would change for the better the lives of most in the room and ultimately change the course of time-sharing from a small, struggling, stigmatized business to the multi-billion dollar industry now prevalent throughout all economic levels in this country. In part, here's what I said to inspire the initial steps of such dramatic change.

"Most of us in this room are veterans of this business. I want to ask each of you, how many projects have you sold for so far?" The answers came, "six," "four," "eight," "five," "six," etc.

"Is there any one in this room that doesn't think you're just great? Yeah, you're all absolutely fabulous. Sure, me too. Then tell me—why is it, if we're so good, so talented, so wonderful, that we live like second-class citizens? Like gypsies, traveling from town to town, project to project? We can't own a home because we're not in one place long enough. We live a lifestyle that no one would chose, yet we continue to deceive ourselves with an air of superiority. Well I don't know about you, but I'm sick of it. I'm sick of living in apartments, a different one every few months, sick of uprooting kids from school, sick of selling myself out of a job when its a good deal, and being stiffed by some bust-out developer when its not. I'm sick of being the fall guy because the developer can't get his act together on a marketing plan. **I'm sick of second-class citizenship**. And I'm drawing a line right here in the sands of Palm Springs, and inviting you to cross it, to join me in a noble experiment—to by God do it right! To recognize that, if anything, we are more flawed than the people we're trying to sell, and begin to elevate ourselves to their level rather than bringing them down to ours. They occupy the real world, not us. We live on the fringe of their world—but we desire to be a part of it.

"I want to develop professionals who realize that this isn't a gallery for sales sharp-shooters, but an opportunity to introduce the public to a lifetime of sensational vacation experiences. I want to create a working environment that combines the stability of IBM with the fast track income and excitement of our industry. One in which you are loved and respected by those you sell, who will return to this resort wanting to take you out to dinner rather than looking for you with a noose.

"And when we succeed, six months from today this project will be half sold out, and Ralph Mann will be forced to make a decision. Will he settle for only the balance of this project thereby losing, within months, what will by then be the most dynamic sales team in the industry? Or will he commit to this industry, to this organization, to the long-term thinking that is lacking in this business, and continue to acquire additional property and work to become one of the most successful time-share ventures in history?

"I tell you today, that I will control the answer, and it will be to develop additional properties. If you are willing to develop a new attitude toward your career, embrace the concept of doing the right thing because it's right and change the very face of time-share, then stay and join me. If not, leave this room now, and save yourself the embarrassment of being thrown out later."

Thus began the climb from humble beginnings to the largest, most successful time-share venture in the USA. The statements and predictions in my "inaugural address" would turn out to be prophetic. I had a vision of where it could go, and this was a classic example of preparation meeting opportunity. Like most success, it wasn't easy. I had endured and/or enjoyed twenty-five years of learning, of trials, and of perseverance that would enable success. But the hurdles were high.

In the first six months with Glen Ivy, I would be required to attend several court hearings in Honolulu. I had been up front about my IRS problems with Ralph in our initial exploratory conversations, so my job wasn't threatened. The attorney, CPA, and travel expenses kept me from having enough funds to settle the debt. It was a catch 22. By then, the IRS was assessing my $40,000 tax debt, with penalties and interest at over $100,000. My final court date was set for January 1984, when the sentencing phase would take place. I expected to receive one year of probation, ending when I paid the tax balance.

Life is full of the unexpected.

* * *

Unfortunately, John Faraone never got the OPC location opened. Ralph had funded the venture with ten grand, which, unfortunately, John blew within two weeks, undoubtedly on coke. I could no longer protect John or his interests. Frankly, I didn't know the guy who had taken over John's being. It was, at least for the time being, a huge loss of one of the greatest talents I had known. He was dumped by Ralph with finality, and left town.

Because of my previous assurances of sales production sufficient to cover cash flow deficiencies, Ralph would often notify me on Friday of the amount of sales needed over the weekend to avoid disaster on Monday. I would do whatever it took, within the boundaries of integrity, to meet the demand, offering cash spiffs and bonuses for performance together with special discounts for the buyers. We made every deadline and never bounced a check. Sales rapidly grew to $1,000,000 per month.

Robin's youthful enthusiasm was infectious. She was a delight to have around. She had secured a job with one of the competing time-share resorts, but kept our relationship hidden for fear it would compromise her job. As the days grew into weeks, so too did our relationship grow more intimate.

She arranged to have her brother drive her little Honda Civic out to visit us in return for flying him back home. He was the first member of her family to get a glimpse of her newfound lifestyle. No sooner was he back home than her mother began burning up the phone lines with questions for her daughter. They were in the process of mending their fences. Her Dad even called. He was living in Costa Rica since his retirement months earlier.

The cat was out of the bag—we were an item. She had a car, a job, and an income. She was in a position to leave but voiced her strong desire to stay. Certainly, I did not want her to go. It was unplanned and unintended, many would argue unwise, but we were falling in love.

\* \* \*

# CHAPTER THIRTEEN
## ~ The Unthinkable ~

For me, stepping off the plane in Hawaii during any season is to enter a surreal world of comfort and content. The soft warm air embraces the body in a welcoming seduction of peace and relaxation. Even stepping into this utopian embrace for a day of reckoning in a court of law was pleasurable. It helped quell the butterflies inside which fluttered about each time I contemplated the worst-case scenarios. I told myself that a deal is a deal, and one had been made with the U.S. Government. What could go wrong? It was, after all, a misdemeanor.

These occasional trips had provided an opportunity to get together with Rick Steere who had attended all the hearings with me. This time, together with my local attorney, we would hear the consequences of my tax-delay decision five years earlier.

I couldn't believe my ears when the federal prosecutor intoned "Your honor, due to extenuating circumstances, we are asking that you sentence Mr. Radez to at least one year in a federal prison…"

I don't know what he said after that, as my mind couldn't process anything that followed "…one year in a federal prison." What? Had I heard it, or were my fears manifesting themselves in a waking nightmare?

About the time I was regaining my equilibrium, he was offering the judge a sworn, written statement from Rodney Inaba, the CEO of Inter-Hawaiian Leisure, attesting that I had embezzled significant funds while in the position of Executive Vice President of his company. He further stated that I had been promptly fired when my evil conniving ways had been discovered, but due to Inaba's kind heart, had not been prosecuted for the crime.

Both my attorney and Steere joined me in shock. None of us had ever heard of this, and it was an absolute fabrication, with obvious ill intent. All objections by my attorney were rejected by the Japanese/American judge who took at face value the assertions of the Japanese/American businessman as presented by the Japanese/American prosecutor. Against this howlie. I was not given the opportunity to rebut the outlandish, completely false statement, nor was Steere, the company's President at the time in question, allowed to refute the absurd charges.

The judge, taking into consideration all the "facts," including letters on my behalf from my children and many others attesting to my good character, decided on leniency. I was sentenced to 90 days in the minimum-security section of Lompoc Federal Penitentiary in Lompoc California, a maximum-security prison, to be followed by one year of probation. I agreed to voluntarily surrender myself to the Lompoc prison in 60 days.

The federal prosecutor had earlier offered a probation only sentence in return for the guilty plea, then, at the last moment, reneged and produced a false document to elevate the perception of the "criminal behavior" as a favor to his friend, Inaba. Even though I was responsible for my attempt to forestall two year's of taxes, this entire legal affair was all about Inaba's vengeful intent over a non-existent wrongdoing. Apparently it had been determined that if the case were transferred to the mainland, the low-level misdemeanor status would warrant only the usual "slap on the wrist", denying Inaba his pound of flesh. It was an actual "conspiracy to incarcerate." Somewhat ironically, I was both guilty and railroaded.

\* \* \*

My prediction for the outcome of the tax matter certainly was off, but the predictions regarding the growth and success of Glen Ivy were spot on. Ralph was on the precipice of deciding to acquire another resort and I was nudging him over the edge. Convinced we had created a formidable sales machine, he realized it had to be fed inventory to continue. In a conscious effort to exploit an outstanding Southern California market, we embarked on a strategy that would eventually be followed by the industry.

Up until that time, there were no major players in the time-share industry. The Holiday Inn's effort was considered a pre-paid hotel room program, and no other national name was willing to take the plunge. Time-sharing was still primarily a method of shedding otherwise failed properties. We chose instead, to study our market, determine what they desired in vacation destinations, and provide such destinations and accommodations that had a predetermined desirability in an all-encompassing program. We determined that the sun loving Californians also loved their snow skiing. Our next project was in Park City, Utah. A small on-site sales operation was developed at the Park City resort, headed by Ron Eckhoff, who readily recognized the unique credibility and direction of Glen Ivy after visiting me in Palm Springs for a few days at my invitation. A Southern California boy, Ron wasn't thrilled about living in the snowy climes of Utah, but I assured him that success in Utah would lead to a more desirable opportunity in his original stompin' grounds.

With the addition of Park City, we adopted another innovation, the use of all properties in our system by the owner/members of any resort property in our system. This led ultimately to our including resorts in Laguna Beach, San Luis Obispo, Lake Arrowhead, and Mammoth California, as well as Hawaii, Colorado, Texas and New Mexico. In all, 26 resorts would be added and sold out during the next six years, accommodating over 60,000 families, mostly in Southern California.

The limited use of time-share ownership had been an obstacle in its growth. We crafted our program to allow unprecedented use and benefits that had not previously been imagined, not only enhancing its value, but also garnering satisfaction rates among our owners that exceeded those of the biggest names in the resort/hotel/hospitality industry. Indeed, the perception as well as the reality of time-share had been positively changed forever.

The extraordinary success of Glen Ivy was due in large part to my experience in the land sales/hospitality room business. After the addition of Park City as our initial mix of vacation experiences, Ralph and I could both visualize the growth that could materialize. The effort to control the cost factors of numerous sales operations spread throughout various states had sunk several predecessors.

I convinced Ralph that major off-site offices located in the large population areas of our market, Southern California, each selling multiple properties, was the solution to realizing our potential. Others had also tried off-sites with limited or no success. Again, costs as well as cancellation rates were disastrous.

I was convinced that with a management compensation program based not only on sales volume but also on overall costs within management control, combined with our uncommon professionalism, together with the growing public awareness of our credibility, plus the superior talent and training of our people, we would be enormously successful. We would require, however, compatible, upscale and credible off-site sales facilities.

Ralph agreed with my vision, and decided to roll the dice for the anticipated $1,000,000 commitment the first such facility would require. But there was a problem. We were into March, and I had a previous commitment in Lompoc. Ralph volunteered to run everything in my absence and put the off-site plans on hold until my return. I could only cross my fingers and hope.

* * *

# CHAPTER FOURTEEN
## ~ An Occasional Rhyme to Pass the Time ~

The apprehension level was off the chart as we drove onto the prison grounds, up to the main building entrance. Robin had made the five-hour trip with me, and would drive my Cadillac Eldorado back home alone. I had offered to send her back to New Jersey, if only for the duration, but she adamantly refused, choosing to take care of the household in my absence. She made it clear she intended to be a permanent part of my life, prison and all other obstacles be damned. Given my enormous debt to the IRS and the uncertainty of the time, I was not inclined to make a commitment even if I could overlook the difference in our ages. I couldn't. We said our goodbyes and, with a deep breath and even deeper resolve, I walked up the steps and through the doors of the drab gray stone building, into a time of great trepidation.

I was processed in and assigned a space in a dormitory. Not a bed or bunk. A space. The dormitory housed about sixty inmates. The guy in the next space—with a bed—felt sorry for me and provided a blanket to mitigate the cold terrazzo floor. The following day I was allowed to scrounge around for a bed in an open storage area of discarded bed frames and mattresses as well as find a locker for my meager belongings. By noon, I was "installed."

In the next few days I was indoctrinated with all facets of prison life, including a job. Various types of work are available for the minimum-security inmates. Some learn a trade at the furniture factory, which produces and markets wooden furniture. A large farm operation provides much if not all of the meat products and vegetables consumed at the prison. The farm requires a long slate of different workers from cowboys to tractor drivers. Numerous people are utilized in administrative functions in the general office duties of the prison as well as medical, legal, religious and other departments. Considered a plum job was the grounds maintenance crew, because they worked outside every day.

I was assigned to orderly duties at the adjoining maximum-security complex. I would be responsible for the daily waxing and buffing of floors, dusting and sweeping and general cleaning of offices on two floors in the administrative area, replacing the orderly whose time was up.

There is no comparison between the two separate prison compounds. The minimum-security area was designed to hold three hundred, but housed nearly five hundred at the time of my incarceration. For those under the false impression that such facilities are federal country clubs, let me be very clear: there ain't a golf course.

There is a track of sorts for jogging or walking. It is a path pounded out around a dirt field by millions of steps of boredom and frustration and anxiety. A crude softball-diamond fashioned by wear and erosion occupies the encircled field. There is a basketball court, a ping-pong table and a bocce ball pit. That's it. And five hundred guys, four hundred of which are wasting their time and the taxpayers' money.

They are all non-violent criminals, mostly guilty (or not) of petty acts of insignificant consequence. Guys doing two or three years for being caught with two or three joints. Certainly, I was the exception, earning over $20,000 per month while there, but what really was being accomplished by my incarceration here? Was I being "rehabilitated?" Punished? Nonsense. If the crime was judged to be trying to cheat the government out of money then why spend taxpayer's money to feed and house me for three months while I gain $60,000 in income? Make me work and turn over the $20,000 per month for three months. Now that would hurt. This was a farce. Nothing positive could come from it. Now magnify my sentence many fold, times many people, and imagine the waste. There must be a better way.

The maximum-security compound was a whole different world. Most Americans don't realize it, but there were only three maximum-security federal penitentiaries in the USA at that time. It's where the truly bad guys are held.

Just getting into the complex was enough to unnerve me, and I worked there. Before entering the heavy electronic gate leading into the compound, I would first have to identify myself to the armed guard in the tower over the gate. He would then locate me on that day's work list before opening the electronically controlled gate, allowing me to pass through three separate razor wire fences.

Before entering the building, I had to remove my shoes and be searched. Cleared to enter, I would pass through a metal detector inside the building entrance, and if it beeped, I was subjected to a strip search. Then I would report to the administrative office and begin my day's work.

On both my floors, I was assigned a small office space for safety in case of the alarm sounding. It was triggered when a fight broke out, a stabbing took place, or some act or acts of violence endangered safety. I was instructed in such events to go immediately into the office on the floor I was working and close and lock the metal door until the all clear was signaled. The alarm sounded nearly every day, sometimes more than once. All administrative members were correctional officers, and all would immediately arm themselves during these events.

I quickly earned the respect of the office staff, mostly women, and was given some slack. The job, which my predecessors had taken all day to do, I would complete in a couple of hours. To help fill my time, the gal in charge let me do much of the filing, and eventually provided me with a typewriter in one of my safe rooms. I didn't know how to type but figured I would never have a better opportunity to learn the hunt and peck system. In appreciation, I hunted and pecked the following.

## A TRIBUTE TO THE LADIES

When I was free out on the streets
And taking count of all life's treats,
I knew which was the best of sweets-
The ladies.
Who brightened up a gloomy day,
And made my troubles fade away?
Who made the night a time of play?
The ladies.
And then I found myself apart.
From all those feelings of the heart.

And in this cold vast criminal mart
No ladies.
The mind becomes an empty shell
In which one is forced to dwell.
A large void in this subtle hell
No ladies.
What undefined but certain things
The presence of a woman brings.
What makes mere peasants feel like kings?
The ladies.
But now I toil from eight to three
Happier than I ought to be.
And what has made this change in me?
The ladies.
Who says hello and gives a smile
That helps me through another mile?
And makes it pleasant all the while?
The ladies.
So please forgive me if I'm frank,
For in this place I have no rank.
But humbly I'd like to thank
The ladies.

Since I would be there only three months, I signed it "The Quarterly Orderly."

I left a copy on the supervisor's desk one morning, and by lunch every woman in the place was my new best friend. They all wanted to know if I really wrote it myself, and each began taking the time to ask about my life. I became a very special inmate overnight—in the maximum-security administration office. "…. I need only come up with a verse."

Each visiting day Robin would make the ten hour round trip to spend two hours with me. I cherished the time with her and realized the depth of her feelings and loyalty. Especially when she smuggled in an Egg McMuffin one Sunday. It defies reason how such a simple food item could taste so exquisite. It also underscored just how bad the prison breakfast fare was.

I was elated to find out that for every four days served with "good behavior," the sentence was reduced by one day. With a little luck, I would be released in 74 days. A day in prison is a long, long 24 hours. It's just plain boring. I spent as much time as possible on the typewriter in my safe room. After a visit from Robin, I would always be inspired to write something for her, sometimes serious, sometimes light hearted.

## DARK DAYS

Please shed not your tears over these darkened days.
For the sun will burst forth and we'll bath in its rays.

The gray skies and thunder, which now are above
Will clear from the heavens and strengthen our love.

And when it is over we'll have much to share:
A love like no other, a caring so rare.

We'll live in its glory and savor the pleasure.
We'll never forget we've life's greatest treasure.

We'll soar all the heights and sing our own song
To our special club only we can belong.

So shed not your tears for the gray skies above.
Very soon they will clear leaving only our love.

\* \* \*

Partitions, such as those used to create cubicles in many business offices, separated the individual sleeping areas in the dormitories. The spaces created were quite small, six by eight feet. But it was "home."

My "neighbor" was a large Mexican I nicknamed "Pancho," whose mustache and general appearance portrayed my impression of Pancho Villa. There was an uncomfortable moment when he questioned me about any derogatory implications, but upon my explanation, he liked the linkage and grew fond of hearing himself referred to with it in mind. Despite his menacing looks, he proved to be a friendly neighbor, although his snoring was outrageous.

Nights in the dorm would have been hilarious if I weren't interested in sleeping. The sounds and odors produced nightly by the snoring and farting of sixty guys crammed into tight places was unworldly. I had the feeling I had fallen into a twenty-hole outhouse and was being serenaded by stereophonic assholes. The shit that was passed off as food three times a day exacerbated the severity of the problem. The entirety of the dorm walls were windowed, and to alleviate the problem to some extent, the windows remained open, adding cold to the nightly menu of loud and stinky. I dubbed Lompoc a "Federal Fart Farm."

Cash was considered "contraband" and its possession was a strict taboo. Unannounced searches of lockers and bunk areas were conducted periodically. In lieu of cash, other forms of tender were used, cigarettes being the most common. I kept a ready supply of different brands, but mostly menthols, the popular choice.

Most in the Fart Farm for any length of time are flat broke with no source of funds, so people in the right places due to their jobs were usually willing to do a "favor" if cigarettes were available. Pancho worked as a cook in the kitchen, and I found within my first 30 days he had connections with inmates in virtually every area of our universe, largely a result of having already been there for over two years. His job definitely had my attention since the food was so bad. He confided he never ate the standard fare served to the general population.

I had resigned myself to mostly candy bars and other snacks available in the prison shop which was open for two hours, three days a week. A personal credit/debit account was established and credits were made for the seventeen cents per hour earned from one's assigned job. Any other credits had to be funded from an outside source. My account was well funded.

All services from mail to medical to the shop required an insufferable wait in line, or arriving two hours prior to the scheduled opening time. Either way, it meant standing in line. Unless you had the luxury of tender—many cigarettes—to offer someone else for standing in line for you. I had an enviable supply.

"Pancho" I said one evening as we enjoyed a smoke, my treat. "Do you ever smuggle special meals from the kitchen for others?"

"No, no," he said. "Too risky. I could do it, but the reward would have to equal the risk."

"What do you think would be the most valuable items or commodities you could have in this joint?" I asked.

"Booze and drugs" was the immediate response. "And certain types of candy the shop doesn't have. Cigarettes ain't gonna get it." He thought he was working me.

"If it were possible for me to have a bottle of booze and, say, half an ounce of really good pot and some special-order candy delivered to you, would that be worth the risk of you getting me a really good steak once in a while?"

"Amigo," he said enthusiastically, "that would be very valuable. Maybe, three or four steaks. But how you gonna' do that?"

"Make it a couple a week for the next four weeks, and I'll make it happen— with your help."

"Wait a minute, amigo. My help?"

"I know you have good friends that work the farm. We'll need just one guy as a 'runner' there to make it work."

"The farm? Why the farm? And another player means more payola."

"Yeah, that's why I'm gonna' arrange for a full ounce of dope plus an extra candy for the runner. Can you get it done for the extra half ounce?" I asked.

"What's a 'runner'?" He was getting into it now. And he hadn't flinched over two steaks each week.

At the far end of the walking track, a narrow stretch of woods separated the track-encircled softball field from the farm. One afternoon I had crossed through the woods to the well-defined boundary of the farm, signifying "go no further." Only those who worked the farm were allowed on farm property.

Still inbounds, my eyes had followed the fence beside the small creek that was out-of-bounds, some quarter mile down the farm line to the nearest road. I recognized the road as the one leading to the prison, crossing the creek over a small bridge some distance from, and out of sight of, the prison. The bridge was a perfect drop spot.

"A runner is the guy who is going to pick up a package under the bridge at the end of the farm property and deliver it to you. You are going to be a hero and earn many favors for giving the guy lucky enough to be your runner, half an ounce plus a special order candy item"

I could see his wheels turning, and I was really beginning to enjoy the cloak and dagger aspect of the scheme.

"Bueno," he announced. "When?"

"Not until you tell me you have a runner committed."

"I have him tomorrow," he said.

"Then two weeks from tomorrow." Tomorrow was visitors' day.

\* \* \*

Damn, she looked good. With me no longer around to feed, Robin had been successful in cutting back on the goodies and had gotten her 5 foot 4 inch frame to a svelte 115 pounds. I could have eaten her on the spot—and wanted to. Other than the perfunctory hello or goodbye kiss, no smooching was allowed. But we could embrace or sit next to each other in semi-embrace.

She filled me in on all the news from Glen Ivy—the problems, the complaints, the concerns from my team members. She answered my questions, and did all in her power to encourage me and lift my spirits. "I just wish I could do more," she said.

"Well, there is something you might do, but it's about food, not business. And only if you're comfortable doing it. I don't want you to feel like you have to do this. It's just an idea. OK?"

I explained the whole situation and exactly what the plan would entail. She immediately enlisted, and with enthusiasm. This plucky lady, who never ceased to amaze me, thought it would be fun. She was getting into the cloak and dagger thing too.

I gave her the list that Pancho had handed me that morning. I had wondered out loud why he had asked only for a pint of whisky rather than a quart, and was told it was too difficult to hide and pass a quart. Of course, the pot was the real deal. Almost as important was the pecan cookies and Rocky Road candy bars.

She would have two weeks to put it all together in as small a package as possible for the next visit to deposit under the bridge on her way back home. She would be breaking no law so I wasn't too concerned about Robin. I would never see or touch the items, so the scheme had little downside for me personally. It was all about ending up with some decent food. And it was a welcome relief from the boredom for all concerned.

The next day, Robin was on my mind throughout the day. I finished my work as quickly as possible and retreated to my safe room and, in a take-off on "Tribute To the Ladies," wrote "M.S.T" for Robin.

M.S.T.

Who makes the sun rise every day?
Who makes my troubles fade away?
Gives me pleasure I can't repay?
My Sweet Thing

Just who is it that loves me so?
And makes sure that I always know
She's here to stay—she'll never go?
My Sweet Thing

And when I'm angry and I speak
In tones one pitch above a shriek
Who understands my nasty streak?
My Sweet Thing

Who comforts me in ways devine
And makes me want to walk the line?
Who lets me know she's mine all mine?
My Sweet Thing

Who makes me want to rise above?
Make her proud and earn her love?
Fits me like a tailored glove?
My Sweet Thing

Who flames my passion into fire
Makes my blood boil with desire
Then satisfies the glowing pyre?
My Sweet Thing

And after making me a king
Knowing I'd give anything
Who is it wants a wedding ring?
My Sweet Thing

* * *

"Hey, Pancho. You sure your runner is on board for the pick up?"

"Hey, Amigo, he can't wait."

"You know, Pancho, that when this goes down, if you don't deliver on your end of the deal, I'll have to kill you." I said it with a straight face but his look was so incredulous, I broke into laughter. Fortunately, he did too.

"Amigo," he said, "for a minute I thought you were loco. Don't worry. This goes down, you're gonna eat good."

The worst thing about incarceration is incarceration. We are so blessed in this country that we take many things for granted, things for which those before us have died. The simple freedoms, the ability to go and come as we please. There, in prison, the food was terrible, the forced company was generally undesirable, and the menial work was demeaning. But the controlled restrictions on time and place and activity were the worst, contrary to our nature.

The combination of these ingredients induces extreme boredom, making hours of minutes and weeks of days. I occasionally attempted to place myself in a mind-set of having a two or three year sentence to serve. It was unimaginable. I don't know how it can be mentally handled. With my hoped for 74 days more than half served, it seemed I had been there forever, and, with only some 30 days left, the time passed so slowly that my imminent release wouldn't appear on my mental horizon. I wrote:

I'm serving my time the best way I can
Avoiding the crying and grieving.
But the uppermost thought that remains in my mind
Is the fantasy thought of my leaving.

And fantasy it does remain,
Bringing little cheer.
No matter how hard I concentrate
Reality is—I'm still here.

I think of the pleasure that waits for me.
The images are clear.
The life I've worked so hard to build -
Forget it—I'm still here.

A giant void I'm caught in
Where each days like a year.
I'm trying to run but my feet won't move.
And each day I'm still here.

I check the calendar, watch the clock.
My objective seems so clear.
All I want to do is leave.
But all I am is here.
I wait for the joy of knowing I'm short,
Knowing the time is near.
But the joy doesn't come—nothing has changed,
Knowing I'm still here.

Will it ever end? Will the time really come?
Do I have a valid fear?
Am I trapped in some strange twilight zone?
Lord help me! I'm still here.

\* \* \*

As always, Robin's visit was the oasis in a desert of monotony. She had become friends with some of the key players in the Palm Springs Plaza, and was able to fill me in on the problems and concerns that awaited me at home. We talked of anything and everything, but this time, we had a new topic.

"Were you able to get all the things on the list?"

"Yep. And they're in a nice manageable package. I'll leave a little early, before everyone else. The road should be deserted."

"Just make sure no one sees you," I cautioned.

"Don't worry about me. Worry about getting your steaks."

We said our good byes fully thirty minutes before the visiting hours were over, and she slipped away. I could only wait and see how it turned out.

That night, just before "lights out," Pancho leaned over the partition that separated our cubicles.

"Hey, Amigo, how you like your steaks?"

"Medium," I said, suddenly excited. "Know where I could find a good steak?"

"In your locker, tomorrow around 5 o'clock."

"How the hell you gonna do that?" I asked.

"Amigo," he said in mock disappointment, "I know people, remember?"

As Monday dragged on in typical slow motion, I kept wondering if it would really show up in my locker, and what kind of steak it would be. I skipped lunch and stayed hungry all day. By the end of the day, I couldn't help but reflect on how incarceration, the isolation from the real world, magnified the importance of minor, seemingly insignificant things. I was certainly no connoisseur of food, just as happy with a hamburger as a six-course dinner, yet I had obsessed all day on the aspects of a possible steak.

While virtually everyone else was in line or on their way to the mess hall, I sat on my bunk, curious how a steak might arrive. At 5:05 a guy I didn't know appeared with a brown paper bag and opened my locker.

"Here," I said. "You can just give that to me."

"No I can't. My instructions are to put it in this locker." And he did.

The bag contained a paper plate, a knife and fork, and a 12-ounce fillet mignon cooked to perfection, accompanied by a baked potato slathered with butter. All still hot.

I sat alone in the peace and quiet of my cubicle, feeling as pampered as if in a private booth in my favorite Las Vegas eatery. My world had dramatically improved. I was able to look forward to this special treat twice each week until my release, four weeks later.

Admittedly, I took pride in having been able to develop and execute a plan within my first 6 weeks that was, for me, risk free and very beneficial. It had also been a lot of fun.

* * *

# CHAPTER FIFTEEN
## ~ "Nothing Is Forever" ~

My day finally came. I walked to the waiting arms of the magnificent woman who had made this trek one final time. This time, she would not return alone. My blue Cadillac El Dorado convertible sat at the ready behind her, anxious to sweep me from this place. The bad dream had ended.

We drove slowly down the coast, drinking in the ocean air, sun on our faces and the wind in our hair. Never had I experienced such an orgasmic mixture of pure joy and relief. It was indeed heavenly. We stopped in Santa Barbara, walked to the end of the pier for my first real meal in nearly eleven weeks—an extraordinary breakfast in an extraordinary setting. It was an extraordinary day.

On the trip homeward moseying along the coastline, drinking in the sweet mixture of breathtaking beauty and unrestricted freedom was emotionally intoxicating and was alternated with the reckless abandon of 100 MPH speeds, the wind screaming in my ears and the radio blaring songs of celebration.

Once home, I walked about the property for several minutes, touching, smelling, seeing the trappings of normalcy seldom appreciated. Then I took Robin by the hand and led her to the bedroom. I meticulously undressed her, piece by piece, struck by the sheer beauty before me. I lifted her onto the bed, shed my clothes and nestled beside her.

I had met her as an enterprising young lady, but I was now in the arms of a full-fledged woman. I pressed my face against the satiny soft skin, held her body tight against my own, soaking in the immense comfort and pleasure of her hot skin, and was conscious of the beginning spiral into uncontrollable passion.

The balance of the day was spent in a suspended euphoria. I was home. I was madly in love.

* * *

My crew was as wildly happy to have me back as was Ralph. Each had a newfound respect and admiration for my management skills. The crew had labored under the admitted ineptness of Ralph as manager, and Ralph was in awe of my ability to so "effortlessly" motivate and manage twenty highly-strung, independently minded professionals. He better understood my equating it to a stable of thoroughbred racehorses. They tend to kick up their heels from time to time, yet each is different and is best handled that way.

After putting out the expected wildfires that had smoldered in my absence, I immediately dove into the offsite project, tabled when I left. I personally spent time in San Diego shopping for the right location. It had to be easily accessible, have ample parking and present a professional image.

Eventually I chose the bottom floor of a new, modern, glass exterior building on the outskirts of town on I-15. This was a make-it or break-it deal. The future of the company or its demise would ride on the success of this expensive venture. I wanted every aspect of the facility and the organization to be first class. "It is not enough to be. We must also appear to be."

The facility would be beyond state-of-the-art. It established a new level of hospitality room environment. From the 15 foot long marble-toped mahogany reception desk through the well appointed but comfortable waiting area, complete with large screen media presentations of snow skiing, tennis, golf, water sports and other vacation experiences, to the theater, equipped with multi-media capabilities together with a stage for the podium presentation, the professionalism was inescapable.

As the facility neared completion, I began to develop the sales and administration team. San Diego had several time-share operations, so a talent pool was existent. Our reputation for success by that time had swept through the industry, and sales reps were lined up to apply. With Ron Eckhoff's help, I was able to accomplish the impossible: convince Ralph that the best person to put the San Diego office on the map was John Faraone, who was back in Palm Springs, clean and sober. I knew if he stayed straight, there was no better person to bank on.

Marketing, bringing the prospects into the facility, is a major key to this type of operation. Frank Braglia was the cleanest, most trustworthy "Unit Broker", or marketeer, in the industry. His two sons had joined him in the business, and I negotiated an agreement with Frank for his sons to supply our San Diego office, with growth potential to other areas of California.

The San Diego office was a smashing success upon opening. With the small Park City office doing $500,000 per month, Palm Springs over $1,000.000 and San Diego nearing $1,500,000, we were off and running. We were close to selling out the Palm Springs Plaza, which housed our original sales operation, so Ralph, devoid of all doubts, worked with me to plan the next offsite location in Woodland Hills. We were also in the process of acquiring another resort in Park City, which had proven to have enormous appeal to our market.

I instructed Ron Eckhoff to select and train his replacement to take over the Park City operation. He had earned his stripes and would head up the Woodland Hill operation that would benefit from most of the Palm Springs crew moving to that new site.

The company's headquarters were located in Corona California, in the middle of the two major offsite locations. My office had been in Palm Springs, but my responsibilities had increased dramatically, and required me to work out of the home office, necessitating a move. As good as things were, I had two monumental personal problems.

I had served my time, but had still not settled with the IRS. I knew that with penalties and interest, I owed them around $80,000. All attempts to discuss the issue were thwarted by them. Cancelled appointments, lost letters, involved agents transferred, etc. It was a huge issue over my head, and they were blatantly squeezing me with glee.

The second was equally unsettling. Robin finally got around to it. She let me know in a calm, rational manner, that if I wouldn't commit to marry her, she would have to reevaluate our relationship. Love or no, she could not spend an indefinite period of her future with me without that commitment.

I loved Robin, but knew better. She was 27 years my junior, younger than my daughter, although they got along marvelously. I was in or approaching middle age (when the hell does that start?), and she was a vibrant, beautiful young woman. We enjoyed each other enormously, our sex life was off the charts, and she was as adventurous and thrill oriented as I. But, ...but ...c'mon, this can't work. Can it? The age difference wasn't a factor to Robin. We certainly were aware of it, and laughed together at other's reactions to it. But …but… no way. Can't happen.

On Thanksgiving Day, I got down on one knee, calling her bluff, and asked Robin to marry me. Calling mine, she accepted. We would be married in the Fern Grotto on the island of Kauai on December 19. We would spend our honeymoon in Hawaii, also visiting the Big Island and Maui during the Christmas Holidays. That solved one of the problems. Or had I gone from the frying pan into the fire?

Some of my friends asked why the IRS, if trying to squeeze me, had not simply garnisheed my wages. The reason was, officially and legally, my salary and total income was $50,000 per year. On a handshake agreement and trust, I was salaried at that amount with the understanding that, as a "patriotic gesture," if I settled with the IRS I would receive a "bonus" equivalent to 2% of sales, retroactive to my starting date, minus the salary I had been paid. Obviously, this was done in the hopes of expediting a fair settlement. Equally obvious, some serious money was being accumulated which I had earned but to which I had no actual legal claim. That, and the fact that I was approaching a $500,000 level of annual income encouraged me to put it behind me.

I called the IRS office in Riverside, inquired what they would accept to settle my debt on that day and was told $160,000. I informed Ralph of my decision to pay, requested that sufficient funds be transferred into my account, had a cashiers check made to the IRS for $160,000 and hand carried it to their office. Without exaggeration, I can say I would rather have had every bone in my body broken with a sledgehammer, and spend a year in recovery, than give them that money.

It wasn't just the amount, but knowing that I had gone to prison for it, how it would be totally squandered by an incompetent government, and that the amount actually represented some $300,000 in earnings after paying the taxes on it.

To settle a maximum tax bill of $40,000, it had cost me $300,000 of income. And seventy-four days.

\* \* \*

As the months ticked by, we not only opened our Woodland Hills office, bringing Ron Eckhoff back "home," but also were acquiring additional properties. Our growth was incredible. We were becoming a known entity in

Southern California. We made a decision to adopt the Muscular Dystrophy Association as our favorite charity, and become involved in various events to raise money for the cause. This association led to many business contacts, further establishing our credibility in the business community. Our well-earned reputation for integrity continued to spread, and the company's adoption of my personal philosophy—"Do the right thing because it's right,"- led to our owner/members rating us extremely high in satisfaction.

"Robin, Son Mike, Magic, Bob"

One of the "crown jewels" in our growing family of resorts was a rare beachfront project in Laguna Beach. We set up a small sales site on the property, but as it rapidly sold out, we secured a huge facility in neighboring Newport Beach for an expanded sales operation. We ended up with over 100 employees in that office.

As my areas of responsibility multiplied, I was named the Chief Operating Officer of the Glen Ivy companies. That officially put me in charge of all but the financial division.

The larger we grew, the more marketing became a major key to our success. With help from the Braglia boys and our excellent reputation, I was able to set up a meeting between Dr. Jerry Buss, Ralph and myself.

It took place in the trophy room at the Great Western Forum, the L.A. Lakers home at that time. I had rubbed shoulders with a number of celebrities in the past, and wasn't prone to being star-struck, although I will admit that spending several hours over two days in our Palm Springs resort with Connie Stevens left me with a teenage-like crush on the sweetest, nicest, most down-to-earth gal ever out of Hollywood.

"Celebrity Guest at the Plaza, Connie Stevens with Bob"

But this was different. It wasn't just sitting at the long conference table in discussions with one of the most famous "movers" in California, awed by case after case of trophies and awards and congratulatory letters from Presidents and other powerful figures. It was the past that I had overcome to get there. It was knowing that two decades earlier, I had run from, or in one case been run out of, town after town, trying to scrape together the rent money or have the electricity turned back on.

This day, I was a party to negotiating a sponsorship for the Lakers that would entail exclusive solicitation rights at all three hundred plus events each year in the Forum, including all basketball and hockey games (the L.A. Kings would sign Wayne Gretsky one week after our sponsorship was finalized), concerts and other events. Ralph was still willing to roll the dice—with proper odds—and we ultimately agreed to a $500,000 package. For one year.

The notable thing about this sponsorship was that no company in our industry had even dreamed of being able to do business on that level. It led to a whole different approach, and again, changed the face of the industry. Within months of that association we inked marketing/solicitation agreements with every major sporting venue in Southern California including the Jack Murphy stadium in San Diego (Chargers), the Coliseum (Raiders), the Rose Bowl (USC), the Anaheim Stadium (Angels), and nearly every other sports site; entertainment centers such as Knott's Berry Farm, whole chains of theaters, the symphony orchestra, restaurant chains and others. We had become very legit.

I worked and/or attended numerous charity affairs in a concerted effort with Magic Johnson, Joe Montana, and other high profile athletes. Glen Ivy became the sole sponsor of an event called 'Night Under The Stars" which raised $500,000 each year for the MDA. Originally sponsored by Ferrari, it was a black tie dinner affair held the first year on the Spartacus set at Universal Studios. The evening's entertainment was courtesy of Frank Sinatra, Julio Eglesius, Lou Rawls and Norm Crosby. It was, by all measurements, a star studded affair.

The following year's event was conducted indoors where Robin and I sat in awe at the adjoining table to then President Ronald Regan.

"Bob & Robin—The Good Times"

With the opening and successful operation of our fourth major offsite, we were selling at a rate until then unknown in time-sharing, averaging $10,000,000 per month. We were a self-contained company, having established our own construction company, architectural and design department, reservations, travel, debt service and financing, all to Ralph's credit.

We bought a Lear 35 jet aircraft which enabled Ralph and I to attend important meetings in distant locations such as Austin Texas (pertinent to our Lake Travis resort), and Aspen Colorado (pertinent to our Aspen ski resort) in one day, saving days of normal airlines travel. The plane was the core of a charter company Ralph created, giving our pilot an interest in the profits of the program. The pilot developed clients such as Robert Redford who occasionally flew between L.A. and Salt Lake City, Tom Cruise and others of the jet set Hollywood crowd. Like all divisions of our company, it too became a profit center.

Our growth was so dynamic we feared losing control, and set aside 1987 as a no-growth year, attempting to maintain the status quo while developing and implementing new systems and policies of control. Even setting aside production priorities, we none-the-less experienced a 25 % increase over 1986.

By 1988 Marriott had entered the industry in Florida, and wanted to open up in California, largely due to our success. At one point Marriott, Disney and Hilton were interested in our company and engaged us in discussions with an eye toward a possible buy out. We needed to either go public or sell to a "sugar daddy" that could fund our growth. We were selling out properties faster than we could replace them. Instead of resort projects with fifty and one hundred units, we needed to develop projects of five hundred units that would provide the necessary inventory.

People sent resumes to me from all across America as knowledge of our success spread. The numerous meetings I conducted with various bank officials on behalf of our Chief Financial Officer would occasionally elicit questions about my education. I always told the truth, citing High School as my great educational accomplishment, to their startled amazement.

"I would have thought you would have an MBA," one blurted.

I merely opened the drawer of resumes, selecting the dozen or so MBA's that had applied, and responded, "I don't have one myself, but those who do are waiting in line to work for me." It never became an issue.

\* \* \*

"Vengeance is mine," saith the Lord. But occasionally, a little of it is too good to pass up.

"Mr. Radez, there's a Phil Danti here to see you. He says he an old friend." My secretary knew I had an open door policy and never hid from any callers, phone or in person. In fact, I even read all mail to the company to make sure I knew of any problems or praises first hand.

I hadn't seen Phil since the land business days when he was playing God at Gulf American Corporation, and belittling my suggestion that professional podiums were an important key to hospitality room sales. I walked out to meet him, greeted him warmly with a handshake.

"Hi Phil. Long time no see. Come on in."

When the company moved into our expanded offices the year before, Robin, who was establishing herself as an interior decorator, asked for and received permission from Ralph to choose everything in my office. Unlike the staid mahoganies and oaks which office designers prefer, mine was done in dramatic fashion with a long crescent shaped ebony desk top suspended on two stainless steel cylinders, with all the matching files, chairs and art that exuded class. It was unique and impressive. Phil tried not to show his wide-eyed surveillance of the room.

"So, what brings you to our little town? Are you still living in Vegas?"

"Well, I'm still living there, but I'm looking for a deal. I know you guys have been on a tremendous roll and can use top notch people."

"What did you have in mind, Phil?"

"Bob, you may not know, but I'm one of the best podium men around, and with the number of rooms and parties you're running, I figure I could be a big asset to you."

"Why, Phil," I said in mock surprise, "you're the one who taught me the error of such thinking when I was helping to increase sales in your GAC rooms. Hell's bell's, Phil, I could put a parrot on a pedestal in front of the room and get the same results as with a speaker." He sat motionless for a brief moment as his recollection of that remark registered on his face. Without a word, he rose from the chair and left.

In retrospect, it was the one shamefully cruel act in my career that I regret.

\* \* \*

The CEO and President of Gulf Development Corporation, a developer of Florida communities, had spent several days in high-level meetings with our top people. GDC was a billion dollar, publicly owned, New York Stock Exchange Company. Shortly before courting us, they had entered the time-share industry with the acquisition of a 500-unit time-share project in Orlando Florida, the largest in the USA at that time. They had designs on becoming the biggest time-share enterprise in America. We already were.

They inked the deal to buy us for $100 million cash in May 1988. Our company owned virtually nothing. They were buying our expertise. We had our sugar daddy.

My extraordinary success with Glen Ivy was largely the result of the knowledge I had gained through the numerous experiences of my life, both good and bad. In a relatively short 5 ½ years, I had been instrumental in leading this company from near bankruptcy to the most successful of its kind in the world, from sixteen employees to fourteen hundred, one resort to twenty-six, $3,000,000 in annual sales to over $100,000,000.

I had the help of many talented and dedicated people, all whom prospered from their efforts. And it wasn't just about money. Needing to delegate some of the load, I had promoted Ron Eckhoff to National Director of Marketing, giving up a half point of my two point overwrite (twenty five percent of my income), matched by the company to pay him one percent of sales. That amounted to a million dollar a year job, with $500,000 coming directly out of my earnings. John Duncan was a Vice-President in charge of customer service, and others also shared the responsibilities and rewards of excellence in performance. This was much more than a job. This was, to a large degree, my creation, my baby. I feared for it in the hands of others who could not know or appreciate what went into its making. Especially with more of the decisions being made by the new bean counters who believed business is simply a cold matter of the numbers, never understanding that the numbers are created through the efforts of people.

Within months, unhappy with the direction we were to take, particularly the addition of a Chief Financial Officer, Peter Giummo, whom I distrusted and did not respect, I decided to retire on January 1st, 1990. The physical and mental toll of decades of stress and unlimited efforts toward my financial goals were robbing my enthusiasm for overcoming new and unnecessary obstacles being created daily.

I had maintained a relatively conservative lifestyle considering my seven figure income, and was financially secure, my lifetime long term goal. In addition, I had acquired stock in our privately owned company, and the buyout had resulted in an ultimate payout to me of nearly two and a half million dollars. Rather than take the full amount, we structured an agreement to pay me $200,000 per year on a five-year consulting agreement, saving a hit in taxes, plus the $1,400,000 I received upon leaving.

California land was a failsafe investment, with values soaring. The house we had bought three years prior for $450,000 was worth $900,000. Having an established significant income for the next five-year period, I had time to capitalize on my wealth. We found three twenty-acre parcels suitable for development, and made the plunge with a basic four-year plan for fruition. My cash on hand would cover the anticipated out of pocket costs, with further borrowing on the property available if the unexpected materialized. I anticipated eight-digit profits within five years. What I didn't anticipate was GDC's sudden bankruptcy, Glen Ivy's subsequent nose-dive, or the California real estate crash, all materializing within months.

* * *

179

Retirement for me was an unqualified pleasure. I was 55, had reached my life's goal of financial independence. I was an avid golfer living on a Jack Nicklaus signature golf course in a beautiful home we had built a few years earlier. We enjoyed the privacy and security of a gate-guarded community tucked into the foothills of the Temecula Valley, an hour north of San Diego. It was a Southern California few could imagine, a rolling, mostly rural countryside, surrounded by thoroughbred horse ranches and avocado farms. Near perfect climate prevailed most every season.

I played golf virtually every day, never able to satiate the 30-year yearning to do exactly that. I rode the hills and valleys of the area on the sports bike that had replaced the dirt bikes several years before. With Robin clinging to me from the passenger seat, we would sometimes wind our way through the Santa Rosa mountains to the quaint village of Idyllwild for lunch, enjoying the mountain air and roads which God must have intended for motorcycles.

At long last, I was truly free. Free to go and come as I pleased. Free to relax and enjoy. Free of THEM. Either I had exited the "fringe," THEIR domain of influence, or THEY had been assigned to screw with someone else.

With golf a priority, I was able to hone my game to a fairly competitive level—a 5 handicap for a brief period—and enjoyed teeing it up with such notables as Fred Couples, John Cook, Hale Irwin and others. A golfer's fantasy of playing many of the acknowledged greatest courses in America became my reality. From Pine Valley in New Jersey to Pebble Beach and Spy Glass and Cypress Point in California to Maui's Kapalua to the best of Australia. It was an idyllic time.

"Fred Couples Admires My 1973 Jaguar XKE Convertible
After a Round of Golf"

\* \* \*

"Bob, did you know that both the CEO and the President of General Development Corp have been indicted by the federal government for fraud?" It was Ron Eckhoff on the phone.

"Oh my God! For what?" I was stunned.

"Their New York sales office sells not only home-sites in their Florida communities, but also finished homes. It seems they were inflating the appraised values of the homes to show a falsified down payment in order to secure mortgages for their New York buyers without any real cash in the deal. That's a federal offense, and involves millions of dollars. They're in deep shit. The stock plunged today from $12 to $4. The company seems to be coming unraveled."

"There goes our sugar daddy," I said. "Any immediate effect on Glen Ivy?"

"Oh yeah. All funding has been suspended. All our plans for new projects have been put on hold."

They were not the only ones to come unraveled. Over the next few months I observed in dismay as Glen Ivy's sales sank from its monthly $10,000,000 mark when I had retired, to a dismal $5,000,000. It became obvious that not only were many, if not all, of the 1400 jobs at Glen Ivy in jeopardy, but so was my $200,000 per year consulting fee. My semi-monthly meetings with Ralph had become a painful ordeal for Ralph, with me berating his ineffectual handling of the adverse conditions.

With nearly all my wealth tied up in various real estate investments, my $200,000 annual consulting fee was crucial to our personal survival. To make matters worse, the recession of the late 80's was finally starting to have an effect on California. When the subject of my return to Glen Ivy was broached, I had little choice. Once again, I would have to take control of the situation. After eight months of an idyllic retirement, I agreed to return for a greatly reduced $500,000 annual salary.

When I retired, I had elevated my top offsite General Manager to the position of National Director of Sales. He needed only to follow my well-established track of success. Instead, he saw fit to change systems and methods, creating turmoil and sending sales into a tailspin. My first act on returning was to fire him for stupidity.

Within ten months from my return, I had reason to be both ecstatic and depressed. My total commitment to re-instilling the "esprit de corps," the company-wide pride in excellence and accomplishment, resulted in a return to the high standards and record sales volumes previously attained. Unfortunately, the mindless interference of Peter Giummo, the CFO, in the sales arena had the effect of placing continual roadblocks in the path of progress. My complaints to Ralph were ignored. The company-wide perception of this apparent "blind-spot" led to rampant speculation that Giummo held some sway on Ralph.

To make matters worse, the brass of GDC had been convicted and sentenced to several years in prison, ultimately forcing their company into bankruptcy. Because Glen Ivy was a viable entity, the courts allowed it to be sold. Ralph bought it back through the court for pennies on the dollar, but still lacked the needed "sugar daddy." And he refused to remove the CFO who, I was convinced, was a growing cancer in the company body.

Ralph was once again the Chairman of the Board, CEO and President of Glen Ivy, but grew increasingly unresponsive to my concerns, leaving me with diminishing control of the company and unable to resolve its pending problems. Full of frustration and empty of patience, I submitted my resignation.

It included for the record, my prediction of dire consequences for the Glen Ivy company if Giummo remained as CFO. Finally even I was beginning to question Ralph's inexplicable protection of Peter Giummo.

\* \* \*

When I had first retired and the world seemed so rosy, Robin and I made plans for "our" retirement. I had often said that if I ever found the right combination of golf course and bass lake, one at my front door and the other at my back door, I would retire there.

Robin had flown to Atlanta Georgia in route to the wedding of a friend in Aiken, South Carolina, a scenic three-hour drive out of Atlanta. She had read of an exceptional golf community on Lake Oconee, Georgia's second largest lake. It was located midway between Atlanta and Augusta Georgia. Aiken is just a few miles across the State line from Augusta.

She took a tour of that property, Reynold's Plantation, on her way to Aiken. She called me that night and said, "If you see this place, you are going to go ape over it." After the wedding, she returned home with all the brochures and literature on the impressive golf community.

We arranged for and spent the third week in July at the Reynolds Plantation. I wanted to experience the worst part of the year climate-wise.

It was beyond the description of the brochures. I believe it was, and still is, the finest golf community in the USA. I loved everything about it. Bob Cupp designed the first golf course in collaboration with noted stars of the PGA, Fuzzy Zoeller and Hubie Green. Jack Nicklaus had designed the second course, under construction at that time. The mixture of the best bass lake in the State, the scenic beauty of numerous ponds complete with swans and other waterfowl, the ribbons of green winding through the tall Georgia pines, the ubiquitous deer grazing peacefully alongside the course—it was all deliciously appealing.

Before the week was up we bought a sensational one-acre home site on the lake, and returned to California to put our home on the market and begin planning our dream home in Georgia. If any comparable site had existed in California, it surely would have been in the two million dollar range. We paid $165,000.

Our home had been appraised at just under $1,000,000, and we put it on the market for $995,000. We owed $300,000 and the difference would fund a fantastic lake home. Unfortunately, the California real estate crash had just started. And it was on a long black-diamond downhill run.

(Through the next half-decade, we would lower the asking price of our home by $100,000 each year, finally selling it five years later for $500,000, giving away over $100,000 in custom made furniture to make the deal. Even more unfortunate, the home was only a fraction of our real estate holdings.)

The call came seven months after my second resignation and retirement.

"Bob, do you have your TV on?" It was Ron Eckhoff.

"Nope, haven't got around to it yet. This old retired fart enjoys a leisurely morning. Why?"

"You're not gonna enjoy this one. Turn on channel 5 and sit down."

The images were so startling it took a full minute to process what I was seeing. The entire Glen Ivy administration staff, some 350 people, were standing outside the company office building in the parking lot, just beyond the yellow police crime-scene tape which stretched around the entire compound. Media people were everywhere, recording the scene of agents from various legal agencies carrying box after box of records from the building into waiting trucks.

"What the hell is going on?" I asked in disbelief.

"Believe it or not, its a goddamned raid!" Ron said. "Three or four different agencies were here before the office opened, wouldn't let anyone in, except every news organization in town which had prior notice of this 'secret' raid. The D.A., who just happens to be running for re-election, has been strutting in front of the cameras all morning, boasting of this operation closing down a major time-share company who was selling property that didn't exist. We're all in the dark. I have no idea what he's talking about."

They confiscated all computers, all records, everything but the furniture, effectively shutting down all operations. Within months, the company was forced into bankruptcy. The raid, the reasons and the aftermath were best explained in a letter I wrote 28 months later, most of which was published in the industry's main international trade magazine under the title "The Glen Ivy Affair—A Time For Truth". It read:

> On an early December morning in 1991, before any employees had arrived for work, a strike force of approximately 100 law enforcement officers, led by the Riverside County California District Attorney, raided the corporate headquarters of Glen Ivy Financial in Corona California. The yellow police tape, usually associated with major crime scenes, was stretched around the

entirety of the one square block facility, and no one was allowed to enter the premises—no executives or any of the 350 employees who worked there. No one, that is, except the camera crews and reporters from various TV stations and newspapers throughout Southern California which had been notified in advance.

While Glen Ivy employees, arriving for work, gathered in shocked bewilderment in the parking lot, the D.A. strutted inside for all the cameras, pontificating on the heinous and fraudulent crimes committed therein. He rhetorically mused why a simple time- share company would need such a sophisticated computer system, the same as used by the pentagon, he said. He vowed to bring in a team of the nations top experts to "break the code" and reveal the true records of wrongdoing. Meanwhile, all records, all files, all computers and back ups, ledgers, tapes, checkbooks, bank records, everything were being confiscated by this armed band of public protectors.

Throughout the following three days, every TV newscast throughout Southern California blared the story: "If you bought a time share from Glen Ivy, you may be the victim of fraud." For 72 hours the media hammered away: Glen Ivy oversold properties it owned and created phony deeds for properties that did not exist; claimed 10,000 Glen Ivy owners were victims of the fraud; marveled at the "Pentagon type" computer used to guard Glen Ivy crimes.

The media did not report: Glen Ivy had an extremely high satisfaction rate among its owners; the company had grown from insignificance in a very stigmatized industry to international renown for its high standards of ethics, fairness and honesty in dealing with the public; never had an unresolved complaint, and maintained arguably the lowest complaint percentage of any type of business in California. Also unreported, was the FACT that Glen Ivy's single largest operational problem was its **antiquated and inadequate computer system**, kept operational with (figuratively) bailing wire and band-aids. (Within two weeks, the D.A. crowed to the media that his team of experts had cracked the code of Glen Ivy's ultra sophisticated computer).

Supposedly incidental to all the above, the D.A. was running for re-election on a platform of cracking down on white-collar crime.

Meanwhile, Glen Ivy struggled to stay afloat. It had no records of receivables or payables; no record of any bank accounts; could not issue any checks; could not respond intelligently to owners inquiries; could not properly handle the reservation requests of its 60,000 owners. Within a few months, all records still under lock and key of the D.A., Glen Ivy was forced into bankruptcy.

Sixty thousand owners were put at risk, 1400 once proud employees were out of work during the worst economic recession in California history, dozens of vendor companies were severely crippled and many destroyed, and the most outstanding and successful company in a world-wide industry was completely devastated. AND NOT ONE CHARGE WAS FILED BY THE D.A. The raid was but a fishing expedition.

A member of the D.A.'s staff revealed that it took nearly eighteen months of examining all the confiscated files, records and materials to develop any significant understanding of the business. Likely, had this "enlightening phase" taken place prior to the raid rather than after, no raid would have occurred.

As the months have passed since the raid, so too have the stories faded from the front to the back pages of our newspapers. The original claim of 10,000 fraud victims was lowered to 5000, then to 3000, and now less than 800. The D.A.'s office readily concedes that only Glen Ivy's Chief Financial Officer is suspected of any wrongdoing. All evidence supports the fact that the sales and marketing of Glen Ivy were exemplary along with the administration, management, travel, construction and all other divisions of the company. All involved agree with this assessment. Yet no report has ever revealed this aspect.

It now becomes incumbent on the D.A. to indict somebody, anybody, or force a settlement by threat of prosecution to cover themselves against the obvious liability of the senseless and reckless raid. No reason has ever been given why the police power of the state was used to destroy a vibrant and successful company rather than taking specific action against those few individuals suspected of wrongdoing. Had such reason prevailed, the lenders and lawyers would not now be fighting over the carcass.

It is a cruel irony that a company which quickly rose to the zenith of the industry on the basis of a total commitment to a superior standard of ethics would be summarily executed by an overzealous bureaucrat without ever being charged with a crime. And worse, that many of those same dedicated employees whose talents and efforts created a genuine American success story are still, after two years, burdened with the misplaced stigma of fraud so freely spread by all reports of this tragedy.

*It's time for the truth. On behalf of all the dedicated people whose efforts built Glen Ivy, the greatest organization of its kind in the world, I offer these chilling revelations.*

\* \* \*

The "fraud" of 10,000 victims, the sale of "non-existent" properties, all concerns that prompted the raid, were easily explained. They need only to have asked.

The 10,000 "victims" were time-share buyers who, after several months, had not received a deed for the property. California law requires delivery of the deed within thirty days. The conclusion jumped to by the ambitious D.A.: the property did not exist.

The reality was quite different. The recorder's office in small communities such as Park City, Utah and Kauai, Hawaii have very limited personnel, and the sudden task of recording 1000 time share deeds per month when a resort in their community commenced sales, was overwhelming. In such cases, the recorded deeds could not be delivered by the recorder's office for six to twelve months. Not only were all customers made aware of this, but also the State of California made an exception to the law in such projects, allowing a full year to deliver the deeds instead of the standard one month. During the course of a year, 10,000 deeds could easily be backlogged. The D.A. apparently overlooked this fact. It took his office eighteen months to figure it out.

By then they were desperate to save face, and Peter Giummo provided their out. He had indeed engaged in several questionable acts, although insignificant in proportion to the damage caused by the raid.

Dealing with thousands of individual time-share buyers with monthly installment contracts, occasionally a buyer would stop making payments and simply disappear. The property itself—and the deed to it—was in a state of limbo. It could not be resold because it was still deeded to the missing owner.

After a year or more of efforts to locate an owner had failed, Giummo had taken it upon himself to solve the problem by forging the missing owner's signature on documents required to deed the property back to the company, enabling it to be resold.

The massive raid and resulting devastation of the nation's premier time-share organization was made without a complaint. After putting 1400 people out of work and jeopardizing 60,000 time-share family owners and creating financial chaos, the raid had ultimately revealed only a small number of non-consequential forged documents.

Non-consequential is apt since, ironically, the missing owners were never located to complain. I am unaware of any other wrongdoing discovered after over two years of continuous investigations.

\* \* \*

The company, along with about $750,000 of my money, was gone. The value of my various real estate investments was spiraling downward in a whirlpool of loss so quickly that selling was impossible. Without the planned income, I decided to become active again, only to discover that the incessant stream of negative and inaccurate reporting by the media had destroyed my reputation. I would have enjoyed a better reception in the industry if I were a leper.

Robin and I were finding California much less hospitable.

\* \* \*

# CHAPTER SIXTEEN
## ~ Questioning the Barriers:
## Insight or Insanity? ~

"What do you know about art?" He was about to tee off on the third hole when he asked.

Richard Gipe was an investment banker and friend, occasionally touting me on some nondescript stock no one ever heard of. He joined me on occasion at my club for a friendly round of golf.

"It's widely believed to be created by artists, although much of it makes me wonder," I replied.

"I'm serious," he said. "Do you have any particular appreciation for art? Paintings, sculptures, that type of thing?"

"I appreciate what some of it costs, though I rarely see anything I think is worth paying for. Well, I'm not really that cynical. I just don't get most modern art. Some of the so-called experts would declare a dog turd on a bed of puke as art if you hung it on a wall. What are you dancing around?"

"My brother and I are getting ready to open a fine arts gallery in Hot Springs Arkansas, and we're toying with the idea of selling serious art across the nation by telephone. Good stuff to qualified people. You think that can be done?"

That was the question that launched our departure from California and our debut into the world of art. But such a launch does not take place overnight. I had long since abandoned Bert DiArmand's credo of "Never own more than you can fit into your Cadillac." Not only had we managed to fill every inch of storage space in our overly-spacious home, but I had floored the attic space over our three car garage which housed the many boxes of who-knows-what that I had been dragging around the country for years. I decided it was finally time to sort through all those boxes and extinguish the nagging feeling that they contained irreplaceable treasures.

Surprisingly, as I rummaged through and discarded box after box, I came across, indeed, a treasure trove. It was a bundle of several letters nearly 30 years old. The letters were from the best friend I'd ever had; a friendship lost which still plagued me to that day. The letters were from Bill Hunter, my dearest friend from the earlier impossible years.

They were written during our days of desperation in the mid 60's, pre-dating any significant success in our lives. At the time of their writing, I had just survived being run out of El Paso, Texas, and was struggling to become a real person in the real world of Austin. Hunter had returned to Las Vegas where he was once again unemployed, existing solely on the income of his wife, Margaret. Understandably depressed, he was expressing his dejection to the only person on earth who could truly understand it – me. As I began reading them anew, I was reminded of the strong bond we had developed through shared misery and failure, and his remarkable sense of humor in spite of it. Being flat broke and unemployed during the Christmas holidays is an especially painful experience that leaves one with deep feelings of remorse and guilt and we shared a resentful disdain of Christmas because of it. Yet as I read of his family's Christmas get-together, I was howling with laughter. He wrote, in part:

"Well, Xmas is gone for another year. We took our tree down yesterday. Actually, I didn't want to put one up this year. I felt that a nice swastika would better express my sentiments, but with Margaret's folks and Grandpa coming down for Xmas, we decided against it. Margaret enjoyed them immensely. It's been a long time since she's spent Xmas with her folks, but I was miserable and embarrassed the whole time, being once again unemployed. Her folks are real nice about it though, never mentioning it. I guess it's like having VD. If your daughter has VD you don't talk about it, now do you. I'm known in the family as 'Margaret's affliction' and when I'm unemployed they just say, 'Margaret's affliction is acting up' and nobody talks about it. They just shake their heads and say, 'poor dear,' and everyone understands."

It was a humorous insight into a humiliating and embarrassing period of life that seemed, like a nightmare, to continually reoccur. Two years earlier, with tongue in cheek, he had penned:

"Today's payday, so if you don't mind, I'll drink a few with you. I've got four left. I do wish Margaret could afford to pay me in cash and let me buy my own beer. I'd buy king-sized Budweiser, not these little ol' cheap Burgemeisters. I don't deserve such awful treatment, not as hard as I work. Bob, you know how clean I keep this house and how hard I yell at the kids. Why, there's not an unemployed husband on this block can yell and scream at his kids like I can. You know that, don't you Bob? I wash a mean dish, I'm good and I know it and so does she. She knows I'm worth more than 6 Burgys a week! But do you think she will pay it? Hell no! I wouldn't mind Burgys too much if she would just buy king-size. I'm not going to put up with it any longer. I thought she would change, but noooo! Every week it's the same: 'Here's your Burgys – be in bed by 11.' ELEVEN, for God's sake! All the other fellows can stay up till 12:00. No More! I'm joining the union first thing in the morning – the AF of L – the Awful Federation of Louses. Some of the other Louses in the neighborhood were seen drinking KING-SIZE Buds after 12 midnight, thanks to the AF of L!

"Shhhh – it 11:00 – I'll tiptoe over and close the bedroom door. THERE, BY GOD! SHE DOESN'T SCARE ME! I'LL STAY UP AS LONG AS I WANT!

Hey, Bob, are THEY leaving you alone? I hope so. THEY're having a ball with me. I still don't know how to fight 'em. If you've found the answer, let me know. 33 jobs I've had in 5 years for God's sake! Isn't that terrible? God help me.

Shhh – I'm going to open the bedroom door now. G'night."

Even though we hadn't spoken in 22 years, I had kept track of Bill through mutual friends. I had been more than pleased to learn a decade earlier that Bill had not only entered a rehab program and reformed his life, but had then become a counselor in the field and successfully maintained his sobriety. I also knew that he had since become involved in a small business in Oregon and was living a healthy and happy life.

A few phone calls led me to his current address in Oregon, and I penned a letter to him. I explained the circumstances that led me to run across the letters and the exceptional pleasure I felt by revisiting the wonderful friendship we had shared. I included a copy of the letters, expressing my belief that they were to valuable to discard, and my hope that he would experience the same joy in reminiscing as I; that I deeply regretted the events that led to the dissolution of our friendship, but that no strings were attached in the sending.

Ten days later, I was thrilled to receive a letter from Hunter. I trembled with anticipation as I opened the envelope, emotions building in me, not knowing what to expect. The totally positive tone of his response brought me to tears. He expressed his great pleasure and surprise in hearing from me, and set the foundation for an immediate resurrection of our relationship. In the following month we shared our feelings on the Reno incident, and agreed simply to put it behind us. Neither of us has mentioned it since. Today, we are very, very close.

* * *

Robin and I would spend 1994 in Hot Springs, learning a new business by applying old lessons. We lived in a home on the shores of Lake Balboa inside the confines of Hot Springs Village, played golf on the five little-known private masterpiece courses available to its residents. A new, separate private country club, Diamante, was being developed inside the community at that time, and our gallery provided most of the art used throughout the clubhouse. As a result, we ended up members of that club for the balance of our stay. I loved the area of Hot Springs, loved living there and know of few places I would prefer for an inexpensive, retirement/golf lifestyle. However, I was one of the youngest people in the Village, making Robin but an infant by comparison. Understandably, she felt out of place.

Even though we still had not sold our California home and were losing or dumping most of our real estate holdings, and could no longer afford to build on our Georgia lake home-site, we decided to move to the Atlanta area.

For a time, it seemed our life was a constant upheaval of moving. We had moved lock, stock and barrel to Arkansas, only to move again to Atlanta. Six months into our stay there, the owners decided to sell the townhouse we had leased, and we were on the move again.

Within a year, we started a retail golf business, catering to women only, and moved again to Alpharetta, Georgia, a suburb of Atlanta and location of our new business. This time, thanks to a series of seminars I had been conducting, and the near give-away sale of our California home, we were able to buy our place and settle in for a time. It seemed we had been boxing and unboxing things forever. The moving company loved us.

The golf business was a great idea in the wrong place. Golf in Georgia gave the impression they had only started allowing women on their courses

15 minutes earlier. Most of the club pros were openly disdainful of women, and the genteel southern ladies had not yet found their voice. While our customers became devoted to us, grateful that somebody cared about and catered to them, there simply weren't enough of them. When our lease was up at the end of three years, we decided not to renew. Robin, however, had become extremely motivated to succeed on her own, and declared that, after living the country club life, traveling the world by private jet, dinning with the rich and famous and vacationing in the glory spots of the world as an observer providing moral support, it was her turn to produce. She entered the real estate field and became a working girl.

After seven years in Atlanta, a couple in the real estate field, Robin was quite an accomplished agent. I had been spending too much time on the road conducting motivational seminars for various companies, large and small. Entitled "The Dynamics of Success," my seminar was designed to provide a road map to help motivate as well as accelerate and improve one's career.

I was more into teaching others the lessons I had learned than in profiting from it. I had studied, observed, worked with and talked to some of the nation's most noted successful people in the assorted fields of business, politics, athletics and entertainment. I had learned much about the quest for success and was eager to share those lessons. As a result, I charged little, spoke often and traveled much.

I had never really warmed up to Atlanta. Our reason for being there stemmed from the dream property we owned in Reynolds Plantation, but we had finally accepted an offer and sold it while in the golf business. It had become too painful to keep, knowing that I no longer had the resources to carry out our plans there.

When, through family and friends, Robin received an offer to move to the Clearwater Beach area of Florida to specialize in luxury, ocean-front properties, I was all for it and encouraged her in every way possible. Before long, we were boxing our belongings again.

Each time we moved, I would find myself contemplating the wisdom of Bert DiArmand—never own more than will fit in your Cadillac.

\* \* \*

Now days, we live on a strip of beach named Sand Key. Its quite unique in that this strip of sand is so narrow, it can accommodate only one street, Gulf Boulevard, and the numerous high-rise buildings it serves. The beach, and blue waters of the Gulf of Mexico serve as our back yard, and across the street is the serene Clearwater Bay. From our 17th floor vantage, we daily watch the dolphins play, chasing boats as well as dinner. The occasional manatee cruises our beach line, as do huge schools of various types of fish.

As I stand, waist-deep in the warm Gulf waters, watching the sunset and casting a silver spoon into the clear waters, the action of the ladyfish and jack crevalles and pompanos occupy my mind. And even when they don't cooperate, I have an incredible, peaceful and magnificent setting to reminisce and to reflect on the big picture.

I've heard so many say, in such reflection, "I wouldn't change a thing." Really? I'd change so many things I wouldn't know where to start. But that is never my mental exercise. I rerun the clips of what was, sometimes mentally rewinding them in disbelief, sometimes laughing out loud at my own ignorance or naivety back then, and wondering about the bewildering cast of characters. Where have they gone? What's become of them?

Ron Eckhoff is living in Las Vegas. Just before I left California, he was in dire need of cash, and told me his second mortgage would be complete in two weeks. I loaned him $5000 for the interim, and two years later, when I mentioned I could use the money, he said he'd get back to me and has avoided me ever since. Ten years after the loan, I found where he was living and wrote this letter to him.

"Hi Ron!

"Sure glad to track you down. I know you must be going nuts trying to find me. I can only imagine how stressful it must have been, all these years, wanting desperately to repay one's best friend but unable to find his whereabouts. Worrying that he might think you're intentionally trying to fuck him.

"Some have said you would be ducking me because you owe me money, but I know you're a better friend than that. Only a low-life asshole would try to stiff his friends. I suppose you've gone to great lengths to find me so that you could repay the debt of over ten years to the one and only person in the world who offered to help when you were down. Even though you were unable to repay the money in two weeks like you told me you would, and despite your knowing that the $5000 was my case money and I needed it nearly as much as you, I'm sure you've been anxious to repay me, probably with the appropriate interest for the ten years you've had the money. At least, I assume that, because I refuse to believe that your many critics were right, telling me for years that you were a complete flake and a worthless scumbag that would intentionally fuck the only decent friend you had. No, I've never hesitated to defend you when your "friends" and associates tried to convince me that you were a worthless piece of shit, not to be trusted.

"You know, Ron, down through the years those who worked with you the closest and longest continually warned me that you were a two-faced back-stabbing bastard who would fuck me without regret, but I said, 'Not me—Ron is my friend.' Over the 25 years that we worked and played together, we shared too many ups and downs, helping each other along the way, developing a deep personal friendship, to ever distrust each other. I know I could never betray that friendship.

"Sharing beans and weenies during the lean periods; pounding the dirt and navigating the sand dunes of Glamus and Dumont on a progression of bikes that, like us, got better and better and more powerful; working our way from the trenches to the executive suites; these are the things that bound us much too close that either of us would ever be distrustful of the other. How rotten would one have to be to violate that rare bond of close friendship? It's that rare bond that establishes deep trust between friends. What kind of white trash would betray that trust?

"Because of these factors, I'm sure you'll be relieved to find out that, despite the extreme personal hardships I experienced, exacerbated by your inability to repay the loan, I've been able to work my way out of trouble. Robin and I are now living in Florida. I'd much prefer to live in California or Nevada, and if I could collect all the money I've loaned to low-life flakes down through the years, I could afford to live anywhere I chose. Of course, when you consider the worthless ass-wipe that I've felt sorry for, and tried to help, I suppose I should expect it.

"But you, of course, are different. You were my friend. And I'm sure that if you had only known how to find me, you could've afforded to pay me a lousy $10 a week which would've paid me back in full by now. But I guess you just couldn't find me because I've never received a dime from you in ten years. Oh, I know others would think you never had any intention to pay me back. But surely you could not be that low, that worthless as a person.

"So now you can end your sleepless nights, wondering how to find me. And to show that I'm still a class act, forget the interest. What are friends for? Just mail the money to me at my Florida home. And in case you forgot how to spell it, its Bob Radez."

Hard to believe, but I've not received any response, let alone money. Gee, maybe those nasty things said about him were true.

John Faraone is living and working in Hawaii. Ten years my junior, he remains in the time-share industry. He was the best. I deeply regret losing our friendship. I hope he's found his way. We haven't spoken in nearly twenty years, but I'd love to see him.

You could say I had the last laugh over Rodney Inaba, although I had no hand in the justice meted out. Rodney considered himself a lady's man, and despite being married, hit on the ladies relentlessly, especially howlie ladies, at the various nightspots. He could get downright crude in this pursuit after a drink or two, and one night while being typically obnoxious, so the story goes, a non-involved howlie gentleman took offense to his remarks. Upon asking Rodney to exercise a modicum of civility, the gentleman was subjected to a barrage of arrogant insults, whereupon he departed, went to his car, retrieved a .38 caliber magnum revolver and returned to shoot Rodney—intentionally—in the crotch. No one has been able to tell me with certainty exactly what pieces of Rodney were scattered throughout the bar, but there is general agreement that, now recovered, he speaks at least an octave higher.

Eileen Cashmere also resides in Hawaii where I first was fortunate enough to meet and work with her. She is the class act of the sorority. We share greetings every Christmas, and I always look forward to her missive.

A.P. Howe called just after I had retired for good in California. He was there visiting his son, was very ill and wanted to return to England to die. He didn't want his last visit with his son to be remembered as him being broke and borrowing money. I gave him airfare and a few hundred to get home.

Rick Wood, while running the Atlantic City operation after my departure, began dating one of the reps, a friend of Robin's, and ended up marrying her and they returned to Arizona. We visited each other often while Robin and I lived in California and they in Arizona. Rick and wife Sheree bought, operated, expanded and sold out a resort in the mountain community of Pine Top Arizona, where they still reside. We communicate occasionally, and remain good friends. I regret that the realities of life prevent us from spending more time together.

Ralph Mann was last reported in Las Vegas, broke. He is the quintessential dumb ass of my lifetime. I built him a financial empire and he pissed it away on a Chief Financial Idiot that virtually everyone else in the company implored him to replace. I'm convinced my tombstone should say, "He built winners for losers."

Bill Hunter and Margaret, his first and only wife, reside in Oregon. They've been married over fifty years. We communicate often, and I love him like a brother. He's the only person on earth that knows the most bizarre events of my past were for real. He lived them with me.

Johnny Duncan is my best friend in life. We speak nearly every week. He's an incredible guy, now 83 years young. He gave up smoking this year—to help his wife who wanted to quit. He's retired, back where he grew up in Missouri. He has a twenty acre gentleman's ranch, virtually all lawn, flowers and trees, and of course, his garden. He tends to it all himself. His birthday is December 7th, Pearl Harbor Day, and every year I tell him the same joke. "I know a fellow whose mother was black and father was Japanese. Every December 7th, he attacks Pearl Baily." We've laughed in the face of adversity together for over 35 years now.

Robin, "My Sweet Thing" Robin, has become a real estate broker, one of the most successful in the area. Our unlikely pairing, believed by most doomed to early failure, has now withstood over twenty years of "…. for better or for worse, in sickness and in health." Simply said, she's one hell of a woman.

The people of a lifetime. The characters, events and places that make memories. But there is one dark cloud that sometimes slips without notice from my subconscious into my thoughts. THEM. Are THEY really a figment of my imagination, a tongue-in-cheek excuse for bad decisions?

I wonder, looking back, could there be a parallel universe, on the fringe of the real world, where THEY hold sway over those who have unwittingly strayed from the real world into the fringe? Do THEY manipulate reality, creating bizarre and abnormal events to thwart attempts to escape, working THEIR madness when escape from the fringe seems imminent?

Mindless blather? Consider—Was the worst labor strike in the history of Phoenix, just as I was establishing a normal life, really a coincidence?

What caused the State of Arizona to put Universal Trailer Rentals out of business in error?

Was an "outside" influence responsible for a meaningless dispute, suddenly ending a simple water softener business in Las Vegas as my life was finding a smooth path?

Was the President of the United States being shot on the opening day of my Denver gold mine yet another coincidence?

Were those my words turning down a Johnny Carson invitation, or THEIR intrusive control over escape?

And when I still managed to overcome THEM and begin building successful organizations, did Inaba suddenly and inexplicably go wacko, or were other forces at play?

Was the Starship subjected to a rash of inexplicable crushing blows because its success propelled me toward the boundaries of the real world?

Could it just be that my enormous success with Glen Ivy took me too close to the edge of the fringe and provoked the ultimate smackdown—the loss of my fortune being the final straw designed to break my back of persistence?

Was the needless and irresponsible closing of Glen Ivy by "Justice" officials a repeat of a tactic THEY had employed once before with Universal Trailers?

Was the timing of California's first real estate crash intended to hold me forever captive in the fringe?

Is it easier to believe that all of these disastrous setbacks, one after another, were mere coincidental happenings, or carefully crafted obstacles placed in the path of escape? Did these events occur only in my universe on the fringe, while the real world remained untouched by such events? What is reality?

I don't profess to know the answers, but remain convinced that there are forces that defy logic and accepted theory.

Suffering the pain and sacrifices to finally make it to the top of the heap, only to lose it all, can cause profound depression. But one of the most valuable lessons I've learned is that the only thing on earth over which we have total, absolute control is—what we think.

If we chose to focus on regret, we will be consumed with regret. Same with hate, anger, fear and other negatives. Conversely, nothing can defeat the power of a positive mental attitude.

And along the way I've learned, just in case, how to deal with the possible reality of THEM. THEY are unwanted passengers on my journey through life. THEY may create an occasional disturbance, even havoc along the way, causing a change in route and untold detours, but I'm still driving the damn vehicle.

Certainly it's been an exciting trip. Today, I enjoy my golf and fishing, and many would envy my circumstances. But even while counting my blessings, there is a void that cries out for fulfillment. An itch that needs to be scratched. I've spent my whole life looking for a deal, negotiating a deal, creating a deal, running a deal. While grateful for the many wonderful people and things in my life, I must admit that one eye is always aware, my antenna up, looking for the next deal, the next project, the next adventure. I quietly yearn for one more opportunity to shoot for the moon. But if it never comes, I know I've already had one hell of a life. It's been a wild ride, unlike any other. Hey! Maybe I'll write a book about it!